Understanding Dyslexia and the Reading Process

RELATED TITLE OF INTEREST

Dyslexia: Research and Resource Guide
Carol Sullivan Spafford and George S. Grosser
ISBN: 0-205-15907-9

For more information or to purchase a book, please call 1-800-278-3525.

Understanding Dyslexia and the Reading Process

A Guide for Educators and Parents

Marion Sanders

Allyn and Bacon

Boston • London • Toronto • Sydney • Tokyo • Singapore

Executive Editor & Publisher: Stephen D. Dragin
Series Editorial Assistant: Barbara Strickland
Manufacturing Buyer: Chris Marson

Copyright © 2001 by Allyn & Bacon
A Pearson Education Company
Needham Heights, MA 02494

Internet: www.abacon.com

Library of Congress Cataloging-in-Publication Data

Sanders, Marion
    Understanding dyslexia and the reading process : a guide for
educators and parents / Marion Sanders.
      p.   cm.
    Includes bibliographical references and index.
    ISBN 0-205-30907-0
    1. Dyslexia—United States.   2. Reading—United States.
3. Reading—Remedial teaching—United States.   I. Title.
LB1050.5 .S224 2001
371.91'44—dc21

                          00-038626

Printed in the United States of America
10 9 8 7 6 5 4 3 2 1   04 03 02 01 00

To
David, Joan, and Rachel

and

To
Steven F. and others
for whom understanding of dyslexia
came too late

Contents

▶

A Note
from the Author

In the late 1950s, I was a special class teacher in a junior high school. In today's parlance, my students would probably have been classified "moderate special needs." They were a mixed group, including some youngsters who were mildly retarded or slow learners, and some of good intelligence with odd or disruptive behavior and poor social adjustment. We had our own classroom and in the interests of mainstreaming, each youngster was also assigned to a regular homeroom class. Those who were socially adept preferred their regular classrooms to mine, and participated as much as possible in the regular program, especially enjoying lunch and gym. Others were shy and fearful in the mainstream and spent as much time as they could with me.

Steven,* an attractive and likable teenager, was in the first group. He was a quiet, well-behaved, intelligent boy, placed in special education because he could not read beyond second-grade level. He enjoyed being with the homeroom group and was painfully embarrassed by his special class membership. He came dutifully to my room when he was scheduled to be there, but routinely checked the hallways before entering, hoping to avoid being identified as a member of this group.

*With the exception of Steven, all other names of individuals noted in case studies and vignettes have been changed, in the interest of maintaining confidentiality.

I had a fresh master's degree in special education from a prestigious teachers' college where I had taken two reading courses, but I had no idea how to teach Steven to read. As far as I knew, no one in the school system had any idea of why he couldn't read. I taught him as I taught all the others in the group, assigning them reading material at their grade level; the assumption was that by following the publisher's curriculum their reading abilities would steadily improve. The other children did improve at reasonable rates, but Steven did not. It was to be another ten years before I learned why Steven could not read and how he could have been taught to read.

I left teaching after four years, but the experience of working with children in the classroom has been an invaluable aid in my work as a clinical psychologist. I first learned about dyslexia from preparing college lectures, but my real education developed over a thirty-five-year course of evaluating children, and occasionally adults, with learning difficulties. Dyslexia was not unknown in the 1950s when Steven was my pupil, but knowledge and practice in that field were confined to a tiny community of pioneer workers. By the late 1960s, there were graduate programs in learning disabilities at a few universities, and recognition of dyslexia spread to a somewhat wider group of professionals, but not to classroom teachers. Today the term is widely recognized, but understanding what it is, whom it effects, and what can be done about it remain limited to a small group of specialists, almost all of whom are trained in special institutes rather than teacher training programs in colleges and universities.

I believe that one reason for dyslexia's not becoming more widely known and understood is that for so long it has seemed like a rare and exotic disease, supposedly with odd characteristics such as seeing words backward. Training tutors for dyslexic students was generally carried out in a few small, private, rigorous, and often expensive programs. Among educators who heard about dyslexia at all, some felt they couldn't afford or qualify for training, and many discounted the entire notion. Training programs were reputed to place inordinate stress on rote drills for learning rules and letter sounds, which struck many teachers as poor pedagogy. In any case, recognition and remediation of dyslexia have for years remained largely outside the province of education in the United States.

The original, singular goal for this book was to demystify dyslexia, to present and illustrate its manifestations so that it will be understood by the public, particularly educators and parents. Although that has remained the major objective, it has also led to a second theme that is dealt with primarily in the last two chapters. We have known for some time that dyslexia is not a present-or-absent condition (like pregnancy or measles) but rather one that extends along a continuum, from very mild to very severe cases. Many children who find reading acquisition difficult manifest a mild degree of the same symptom clusters that characterize dyslexia. These children do not have problems severe enough to warrant a diagnosis of dyslexia, and they generally do not receive special reading help at school. Many fall behind in their early school years and never catch up.

The 1990s witnessed two major developments in the national perspective on reading. The results of a large government research program on dyslexia and normal reading development began to be integrated, published, and made accessible to the public through the popular press, while at the same time falling reading scores in U.S. schools became a matter of nationwide concern. Research results indicate that a large proportion of the children whose reading levels are below par manifest the same clusters of underlying skill deficits that characterize dyslexia. Thus we have a convergence of interests: understanding normal reading acquisition and what can go wrong with it is important both to those who work with identified dyslexic children and to those who are responsible for teaching the vast majority of children to read. The now-doubled objective of this book is to enhance the understanding of the many interested parents and professionals who want reading to be an efficient tool and a pleasurable experience for all children.

Acknowledgments

Many colleagues have contributed to the preparation of this book. Parts of the manuscript were read by Kathleen Atmore, Sue Chollet, Sally Grimes, Dalia Katz, Jess Morris, and Marilyn Ritholz. Rosemary Bowler and Nancy Kates provided thoughtful suggestions about content in addition to excellent editorial work. Jeanne Chall gave considerable time and thought when she read an earlier version of the entire manuscript and responded with very useful comments. Carol Chomsky generously offered to review the entire manuscript and made suggestions that added clarity and accuracy at several points. The peer reviewers of the manuscript, Joyce S. Choate, Carole Spafford, and an unnamed reader, made many helpful recommendations that were of great assistance, and I am very appreciative of the guidance they offered.

▶ 1

Demystifying Dyslexia

Everyone believes in the importance and value of reading. Reading competency is essential for school success and almost all employment; inadequate reading ability puts youths at high risk for school dropout followed by failure to develop satisfying, self-sufficient, and productive lives. Beyond the importance of reading as a survival skill in the modern world are the wonderful pleasures it offers, making it as universal an object of appreciation as beautiful sunsets and a happy childhood.

A large proportion of children who receive instruction in any of the reading programs used in the primary grades learn to read fairly readily. Indeed, some first-grade children have already taught themselves to read by the time they enter school. Of those who don't catch on to reading easily, many will become comfortable readers with a little extra help or extra time. The others—estimates range from about 5 to 20 percent (Lyon, 1998; April 28)—will continue to have some degree of reading difficulty—minimal to severe—for many years and often for life. Among them are those who cannot read at all, those whose reading skills never get beyond fourth-grade level, those who struggle without enjoyment to read what they have to, and those whose reading difficulties do not significantly interfere with their desires but who find themselves reading slowly.

Many, perhaps most, of these children have some variety and degree of dyslexia. Dyslexia is not a monolithic entity; different kinds of skill deficits can cause dyslexia, and degrees of dyslexia range from very mild to very severe. In fact, there are even "normal" readers who show a very mild dyslexic pattern, so mild that it interferes hardly at all with their reading competence. The term *dyslexia,* which means faulty reading, has become increasingly familiar in the last twenty years or so, although the nature and characteristics of dyslexia are not well understood by the public. There are many misconceptions about dyslexia, resulting in both underdiagnosis and overdiagnosis of the condition, and failure to identify and help literally millions of people. While reading experts and researchers struggle to establish a precise definition of and diagnostic criteria for dyslexia, at this time we do know and agree on enough to provide educators, other professionals serving children, and the general public with far greater understanding than they now have. It is time to demystify dyslexia, and to understand how it is similar to and different from normal reading abilities.

Two different definitions of dyslexia are currently recognized within the profession, a narrow one and a broad one (see Appendix A). The narrow definition restricts use of the term to difficulties in word identification, the ability to correctly read words in isolation. This is sometimes referred to as the more mechanical aspect of reading, as distinguished from reading with comprehension. The broad definition of dyslexia includes difficulties with word identification, reading comprehension, associated difficulties in spelling and writing, and a wide range of difficulties with spoken language. Another way to express the difference between the two definitions is that the narrow version deals with "pure dyslexia" and the broad version deals with a wide gamut of language-based difficulties, including pure dyslexia. As it now stands, the broad definition makes dyslexia synonymous with reading disability. The researchers in dyslexia formulated and prefer the narrow definition, while practitioners developed and are more likely to use the broader one. The difference between the two definitions seems to be essentially a semantic one of how the term should be assigned, rather than a theoretical disagreement.

Throughout this book the term dyslexia is used in its *narrow* sense, indicating problems in word identification—that is, the more mechanical side of reading. When the broad sense is intended, the term *reading disability* is used. Difficulties with reading comprehension are addressed separately in Chapter 5, and other impediments to reading are discussed in Chapter 4, but the main objective of this book is to provide an understanding of the difficulties posed by dyslexia when viewed against the background of normal reading acquisition.

Learning the mechanics of reading is a technical skill, analogous to learning to play a musical instrument, or learning to play a sport. All of these activities depend on a combination of sensory perceptions and memory, and the capacity to integrate these components in well-coordinated activity. Although music and athletic activities have large components of touch and movement that reading lacks, all of them are similar in important aspects of initial learning: elementary information is presented, which leads to development of basic skills, and these skills are practiced to a level of mastery that allows them to operate as if on a kind of automatic pilot. In music, one learns to read notes on paper and simultaneously find their sound equivalents on the instrument. In baseball, one learns the rudiments of catching and throwing a ball, coordinating tracking of the ball with body movement. In reading, one learns the names of the written letters and the sounds associated with them, and how to connect those sounds as they occur sequentially in words.

Most people, given some instruction, can learn to do all these things. Some may have special talents, demonstrated in exceptional performance at an early age or catching on very quickly once given instruction. Others show notable weaknesses that make it difficult to acquire the most elementary skills. Children who have trouble learning to play an instrument are often said to have a "poor ear." Those who have trouble with the balance or coordination required for athletics may be labeled clumsy. Those who have trouble perceiving the individual sounds in words, or noticing the sequence of letters when they read, or immediately recognizing whole words accurately, are struggling with some degree of dyslexia.

In addition to their similarities, skill acquisition in reading differs from skill acquisition in music and sports in two important ways. The first difference is the length of time required. Reading skills reach their ceiling at an early age, with normal readers generally mastering the technical elements by the end of second grade (Snow, Burns, & Griffin, 1998). The skill requirements of sports and music require continued learning and practice for a far longer time, in large part because these skills depend on increasing levels of speed, strength, and accuracy, which develop with physical maturation. In reading, the technical skills are within the competencies of 8-year-olds. Afterward, progress in reading comes as a result of growing vocabulary, information, and conceptual development. The second difference lies in the relative social importance of these skills today. Inability to read well puts children at risk for educational failure, which in turn opens the door to a wide spectrum of social, psychological, and economic disadvantages. In contrast, mastering a musical instrument or athletic activity is rewarding but not essential for comfortably making one's way in the world.

Having weak skills for mastering the mechanics of reading doesn't mean that one cannot learn to read. Rather, it means that students with mild difficulties will require more time and practice to achieve mastery, and those with more severe difficulties will require more specialized and intensive instruction. Given the current level of research-based knowledge among reading disability experts, it is well within our means to help those to whom reading does not come easily, but it will be hard to achieve this aim if dyslexia remains misunderstood both inside and outside of schools.

Once there is greater understanding of what dyslexia is and how it affects one's aptitude for learning to read, we can look forward to increased awareness that dyslexia is an eminently treatable condition. We will see that schools can do a great deal to enhance the reading abilities of weak readers, including those whose difficulties are not severe enough to earn them a formal diagnosis of dyslexia. Although some severe and easily identified dyslexics receive appropriate treatment, many at-risk and failed readers continue to flounder in regular classroom programs—their difficulties untreated—because they go unrecognized or because remedial help is unavailable. Reading failure rates have been very high in recent years. In 1994, more than 40 percent of children tested on the National Assessment of Reading Proficiency failed to meet basic levels of proficiency, and it appears that up to half of that number may be handicapped by dyslexia (Fletcher & Lyon, 1998).

Lacking an adequate understanding of what causes reading problems but wanting to prevent or treat them, parents and teachers have had to rely on whatever information comes their way. Much of this information has reflected the current philosophy as reported in the media or practiced in local schools, along with commercial reading programs available through mail order or local tutoring franchises. As parents and teachers understand how children learn to read and why some fail to do so, they will be better able to establish rational and effective reading programs in schools.

We begin in Chapter 2 with a consideration of the normal or usual process of learning to read. Unless we have some idea of what underlies normal reading acquisition, it is very difficult to grasp what it is that goes awry in dyslexia. Although we ourselves have traversed the road to reading, generally we do not recall the steps we went through. We were young, it was a long time ago, and perhaps most importantly, we have become so accustomed to effortless reading that the steps in learning have been fully integrated into the final outcome (fluent reading), so that we are no longer aware of them. We do retain some vestigial remnants of those earlier reading stages, though, and these can help us to understand the experiences of new readers as they develop reading skills.

In Chapter 3 we discuss the outstanding characteristics of dyslexia, one of a number of learning disabilities. The chapter begins with a discussion of factors that characterize all learning disabilities. As awareness of learning disabilities has become more widespread in the last thirty years, the absence of a clear definition has contributed to the prevalence of a number of misconceptions about it, which are also discussed in this chapter. The discussion of dyslexia itself begins with a brief history of the gradual recognition of the disorder over the past century and the pioneering work of Samuel Orton. The specific weaknesses that characterize dyslexia are then categorized and illustrated, standing in contrast to what has been presented in Chapter 2 about normal reading acquisition. Finally we consider the wide spectrum of dyslexia across the population as it comes to light at the time of school entry and in later grades.

The next two chapters take up other impediments to reading. Chapter 4 samples a broad range of circumstances that frequently interfere with learning. We look at situations that trouble many children and families and that, in combination with dyslexia, can turn a mild disability into a serious school problem. Following the framework of Erik Erikson, these circumstances are grouped into biological, social, and psychological factors and focus on the particular matters of temperament, attention, family support, school support, emotional disturbance, and motivation.

Chapter 5 is devoted to reading comprehension problems, the other major source of reading difficulty. While the causes of dyslexia are rooted in neurological functioning, difficulties in reading comprehension stem from many factors, operating alone or in concert. Dyslexia itself is a direct and obvious impediment to reading comprehension, as you first must identify the words in a written communication before you can understand its message. There are also other learning disabilities that interfere with understanding the meaning of text, even when the reader can read with great accuracy and fluency. However, it has been my observation that difficulties in reading comprehension most often stem not from learning disabilities, but from a poor fit between the reader's interests and prior knowledge on one hand, and the content and style of the reading matter on the other.

Chapter 6 is composed of case studies of five children, an adolescent, and an adult whom I saw for evaluation of their learning difficulties. They have varying degrees of dyslexia, and are variably blessed or burdened by their personalities, school and family supports, and the presence or absence of other handicapping conditions. They put human faces to the material that has come before, they illustrate the complex interplay of personal and situational factors along with good or bad luck, and they make clear how important it is to identify and treat dyslexia as early as possible.

In Chapter 7 the focus shifts from the particulars of dyslexia to consideration of how reading is taught in the schools. The schools play many roles in relation to dyslexia, the most obvious having to do with identification, assessment, and remediation. If they were successful in finding and treating every case of diagnosable dyslexia, they would be dealing with perhaps 5 percent of the school population. But there is a far larger segment of the school population—estimates run as high as 50 percent (Lyon, 1997)—who will have difficulty learning to read unless they receive direct phonics instruction—that is, explicit instruction in learning the letters of the language, and the sounds they make in various combinations.

Chapter 7 begins with a brief history of a major conflict among reading educators that has gone on for more than a hundred years. In what some have referred to as the "Reading Wars," there has been a continuing argument between those who insist on the importance of direct phonics teaching, and those who believe that teaching phonics in isolation is not only unnecessary, but is hard, boring, and alienates children from reading. The most recent battle in this long-standing war has centered around the Whole Language Movement, which dominated reading instruction through much of the 1980s and 1990s. We are now seeing another shift in attitudes about reading instruction, due in great part to better research information and growing public concern over poor reading scores. Following this historical review, the chapter goes on to summarize major research findings on reading and reading difficulties, and closes with ideas and recommendations for putting what we have learned into practice.

Chapter 8 continues the theme of "what we can do," taking up a variety of ways in which parents and teachers, schools, and other institutions can play a role in the prevention, amelioration, and treatment of reading difficulties. Major topics include the contribution parents can make in providing a home environment that is rich in literacy-enhancing materials and activities; the preventive power of early identification and intervention during the early school years; and the nature of multisensory techniques used in teaching students with moderate and severe dyslexia.

Educational practice in most schools currently lags behind research-based knowledge about what makes reading difficult for some children and what can be done to help them become successful readers. It will take strong commitment to make changes in teacher training programs, publishers' reading instruction materials, and the allocation of school resources. Knowing that we can prevent or ameliorate dyslexia and recognizing the personal and societal costs if we fail to do so are powerful incentives for change.

▶ 2

Normal Reading Development

Reading comes fairly easily to most people. Not as easily as speaking, because reading requires some organized instruction and practice, but nevertheless pretty easily. Most people learn the mechanics of reading through school instruction in the early primary grades, but there is a broad range of variability among individuals. Some children teach themselves to read by kindergarten age, and others, those with dyslexia, have a difficult time of it, even with special instruction.

Dyslexic readers go through the same sequences and processes of learning to read as normal readers. But they are slower to make their way along the path to fluent reading, and they get stuck at certain places along the way. Not all dyslexics get stuck at the same places, or at the same number of places, or with the same degree of difficulty. But there are certain kinds of difficulty that characterize dyslexia, which, when identified and subject to remediation, can be overcome. With intensive, specialized instruction, almost every dyslexic child can learn to read. How they are enabled to read will be covered in the following chapters.

We will look first at what allows most people to read without heroic efforts. Knowing the skills that normal readers bring to the task makes it easier to understand the impediments to reading that dyslexic readers must overcome. What children bring to the process can be distinguished from what and how they are taught. While both sides of the learning process are critical, our first concern is to understand what competencies most children bring into school with them. Knowledge on this subject has grown at an extraordinary rate in the last twenty years or so, largely as a result of advances in neuroscience and cognitive psychology that allow for more sophisticated and well-controlled studies than were possible earlier.

In this chapter we will discuss only the mechanical, or decoding, aspect of reading—that is, the ability to correctly identify words on the page. Another critical aspect of reading competence is the ability to understand what is read. This is most commonly referred to as reading comprehension, and it is the subject of Chapter 5.

To lay a foundation for the discussion of the normal acquisition of decoding competence in this chapter, we first consider three important topics: the relationship of reading to spoken language, the importance of automaticity in reading, and a developmental principle of psychologist Heinz Werner.

THE RELATIONSHIP OF READING TO SPOKEN LANGUAGE

Long ago when our ancestors began to represent their spoken words in a graphic form, they used pictures or other visual marks. Whatever form was used, it represented an idea or several ideas (perhaps a deer, or a deer running, or a deer running away from something). As written representation of language became more extensive and complex, the number of symbols required reached the thousands, and expressing the relationships between ideas was very difficult. The Phoenicians are credited with being the first to develop a more efficient way of relating written language to spoken language. Instead of using a symbol to represent a word or idea, they used symbols to represent the sounds that made up spoken words. There is a finite number of speech sounds in any given language, so that by using a limited set of symbols to represent these sounds, all words and ideas in the language can be represented. For example, instead of drawing a picture of a cat, we can use symbols to represent the *sounds* in the word "cat." The sounds heard in a word are called *phonemes*. In "cat" there are three phonemes. If you pronounce the word in a slow, stretched-out way, you can hear three phonemes sounding something like "cuh-aah-tuh" (but the consonant sounds are really much shorter than can be represented here in writing). Throughout this book, phonemes will be printed between two slashes, and letter names will be printed between single quotation marks. Thus, the word "cat" is written starting with the letter 'c,' and the first sound you hear in the word is /c/.

The symbols used for representing sounds in the English language make up our alphabet, and the concept of using alphabet letters to represent sounds is referred to as the *alphabetic principle*. English does not have complete, unambiguous letter/sound correspondence—that is, some letters designate more than one sound and some sounds are represented by more than one letter. This makes the task of learning how sounds are represented in writing quite complex. The letter 'c' is a good example of the complexity. It sometimes represents the sound that is also made by the letter 'k' so that the beginning sound in the words *cat* and *kitten* are the same; and it sometimes represents the sound made by the letter 's' so that the beginning sound in the words *center* and *soap* are the same.

The written letters of the alphabet, singly or in combination, make up *graphemes*. A grapheme is a letter or combination of letters that represents a speech sound (phoneme) in our language. The word *cat* has three graphemes. The letter 'c' is a grapheme that represents the sound we hear at the beginning of *cat*. In English, we use the twenty-six letters of our alphabet to make up the graphemes for more than forty phonemes. (For a number of reasons, including the variety of accents and pronunciations, the exact number of phonemes is hard to pin down.) Each of the consonants in the alphabet represents a phoneme, and some pairs of consonants, called *digraphs,* make up other phonemes such as the sounds /sh/ and /ch/. Thus, the word *chat,* which has four letters in it, has only three phonemes and graphemes (ch-a-t). You can see the logic of the term *digraph,* in that two graphic symbols are used to create one grapheme. Most readers respond to 'ch' correctly without actually being aware that the sound is quite unlike either /c/ or /h/. In distinction from digraphs, reading also requires the recognition of *consonant blends,* in which two or three consonants occur together but each one sounds essentially as it does when it stands alone. You can hear the /p/ and the /l/ in the word *plan,* and you hear all three consonants at the beginning of the word *struck.*

Single vowels each represent more than one phoneme: Consider the varying sounds of 'a' in *cat, father, law, save,* and *care.* And a number of vowel combinations represent other vowel sounds: *boat* and *mope, seat* and *feel, pie* and *dye, bake* and *steak, due* and *through.*

So we see that one grapheme can represent more than one phoneme—for example, the letter 'a' is used to stand for a number of different sounds, and as we have already noted, the letter 'c' is sometimes sounded like a 'k' and sometimes like an 's.' Conversely, one phoneme can be represented by many different graphemes. Consider:

- the /f/ sound in these words—*fix, phone, laugh,* and *stuff;*
- the /ee/ sound in these—*meet, seat, receive, believe, concede.*

This lack of one-to-one correspondence between phonemes and graphemes accounts in large measure for the relative difficulty in learning English reading and spelling, compared to some other languages—Spanish, for example—which are more consistent and predictable in their grapheme-phoneme pairs.

Learning the sounds represented by printed letters and letter combinations is often referred to by reading educators as mastering the code or breaking the code, and it is this process that is summed up by the term *phonics. Decoding* is the process of going from the written word to its "spoken" or heard or auditory counterpart. Of course, proficient readers do not actually voice the material they are decoding, unless they are reading aloud. But many people, when reading silently, can identify an inner voice that maintains a stream of auditory imagery as they read.

AUTOMATICITY

Automaticity (the accent is on the fourth syllable) is the desired operational state, the ultimate goal for the decoding aspect of learning to read. We want the reader's decoding ability to become so easy and efficient that it eventually operates on a kind of automatic pilot, with decoding operations moving so smoothly on their own that the reader can devote full attention to the *content* of what is being read.

In this regard, learning to read is comparable to learning to drive a car. The new driver has to learn a number of facts about the car's operation, become familiar with the placement of pedals, gearshift, and steering wheel, learn to coordinate the movements of hands and feet with each other and with the road conditions, and so on. At first this requires full concentration, and is carried out with *conscious verbal mediation* (rather like talking to yourself, aloud or silently), and close attention to the elements of the process. The new driver has to think about each element and movement—where is the brake, which is first gear, when do I put the clutch in, and so on.

As time goes on and the driver gains experience, things begin to fall into place, hands and feet move to the right spot as if by themselves, and eventually the driver is paying little attention to the technical aspects of running the car. She now handles that at a different level of intellectual function: the automatic-pilot level. Instead of focusing on driving, she can simultaneously devote conscious attention to other things: the shopping list, the trouble at the office today, vacation plans, or the conversation with her passenger. The careful driver keeps just enough attention for oversight of the automatic pilot, so that if driving conditions change—for example, a patch of foggy road, icy conditions, or the need to get quickly to the right-hand lane to exit the highway—she can shift into conscious attention for driving. If conditions are very demanding, she may even ask her passenger to stop talking for a moment so that she can concentrate totally on driving.

Automaticity means essentially going on automatic pilot, doing things without consciously thinking about them, accomplishing tasks for which one's brain has now developed well-established routines that need only to be stimulated in order to carry out their functions automatically. If not enough attention is paid to variations in the routine, it may complete itself without accomplishing the task of the moment. For example, if you routinely drive to a certain destination, and today your route to another place starts out on your regular path, you may occasionally become so absorbed in whatever else you are thinking about, that you suddenly realize, too late, that you have followed the old, habit-formed path automatically, beyond the point where you should have turned off (and turned off your automatic pilot) for today's destination.

Developing automaticity in decoding is of the utmost importance for fluent and accurate reading. Just as the beginning driver must understand and get accustomed to pedals, gearshift, steering, and so on, the beginning reader must deal with the symbols that make up our written language, including letter names, letter sounds, a sizable number of whole words, and punctuation signs. He must learn to recognize them, understand their functions, remember them when he comes upon them in print, and in the end do this easily and automatically enough to allow him to devote all, or nearly all, of his attention to absorbing and integrating the content of what he is reading.

We can think of the road to automaticity as having four stations or reference points along the way: The first is the starting point, and can be thought of as a state of *innocence,* in the sense that the individual is innocent of any recognition of how to accomplish the task at hand. This is probably rare in the two situations we have considered here; the beginning driver has been riding with adults for many years and surely has noticed and learned something about the elements that must be mastered. And the child arriving at school for reading instruction almost always knows something about letters, words, and the nature of print.

The second station on the road to automaticity is *cognition,* the point at which understanding of the concepts and awareness of the material to be learned are in place, but successful performance has not yet been achieved. Children generally come to the task of learning how to read when they are beyond the stage of total innocence, but have not yet developed adequate understanding of how reading works, or the variety of elements involved. Reading instruction in school broadens their understanding of how the written words relate to spoken language and provides a sequence of letters and words to be learned, moving from the most simple, frequent, and familiar to the more difficult and complex. Between stations two and three, children practice the essential elements of reading— phonics, sight words, and connected text—increasing proficiency to the point of mastery.

The third station is *mastery.* When it has been gained, the reader knows the basic elements of the language, and can read with a high level of accuracy materials that are within his conceptual grasp and his spoken vocabulary. The major difference between mastery and the ultimate goal, automaticity, is that mastery implies the continuing need for conscious attention to the activity. Additional practice, beyond the level of mastery and sometimes referred to as *overlearning,* will be required to reach the final destination, *automaticity.*

WERNER'S DEVELOPMENTAL THEORY AND ITS RELEVANCE TO READING ACQUISITION

Heinz Werner (1890–1964) was a gifted psychologist and one of the early leaders in the field of developmental psychology.

He was widely recognized in Europe and the United States for his pioneering investigations into the nature and processes of human development and is probably best known as the author of an outstanding work, *The Comparative Psychology of Mental Development* (Werner, 1957a). Among his most significant contributions is the *orthogenetic principle of development* (Werner, 1957b), which has many roots in biological observations and theory. It holds that our mental development proceeds through three stages:

Stage I is *global,* and whole qualities are dominant;

Stage II is *analytic,* and perception is directed toward parts;

Stage III is the final stage, in which parts become *integrated* with respect to the whole.

The progression of stages is applicable to all learning. In considering reading acquisition, this sequence of steps offers an exceptionally useful framework for understanding the process and for evaluating the level and the nature of reading skills that a youngster has achieved at any particular time. There is no indication that Werner thought particularly about the three stages in regard to reading; they are presented here as a framework for understanding the process of reading acquisition, rather than as reading theory.

During the first, global stage, feelings often play a large role, and one's perception is strongly influenced by the context in which it is embedded. It tends to focus on direct sensory impressions, and to draw on personal experiences and associations. Later, in the second stage, as the setting or task becomes more familiar, details begin to emerge or to be noticed in a more objective way, and there is a tendency to give more analytic and formal attention to details. In the third stage, that of integration, the details are seen in relation to each other, and in relation to the whole. It is often helpful to think of Stage III as a return to the holistic perception of Stage I, but this time with a deeper and more analytic understanding of the role and relationships of parts.

Before applying the three stages to reading acquisition, let's begin with a daily-life example of this principle. You arrive at a place you've never seen before: an art museum, a city, a university campus, a hospital. Let's consider a city. At first, as you try to grasp "What is this place?" you are aware of global qualities that affect your senses and emotions: size, color, pleasing or unpleasing, similarities with other cities you have known, and so on (Stage I). As you spend time there, you become aware of elements such as particular historic places, major streets, the location of your hotel (Stage II), and eventually, if you stay long enough, you build up a more comprehensive, integrated notion of the place and its elements and the relationships among them (Stage III). You develop a holistic sense of the place, but unlike your Stage I impressions, this now includes more discrimination and appreciation of the parts that make up the whole.

Stage I Reading—Global, Holistic Reading

And now to reading. In considering the decoding aspect of reading, the word is the whole, and the letters are the parts. For most children, reading begins with words. Although many can recognize and recite alphabet letters, their awareness of print as meaningful communication tends to begin with whole words. Thus, it is when the child recognizes his own name, or STOP on a street sign, that he is most likely to experience the excitement of "I'm reading!" What the child perceives and recognizes at this stage of reading—Stage I—is a global, holistic entity that may be distinguished by certain features, but that he does not analyze by component letters. Thus, a child who can read STOP in this global manner would not be able to use his knowledge to read "top," for he is still unaware that the symbol S represents the sound /s/, that T says /t/, and so on. Rather, his awareness that this says STOP is akin to his awareness that this object is a book and that one is a chair. He recognizes a word as a whole item or object and has learned to associate that item with a certain label. This is reading by way of global, holistic recognition. It is aided by the context in which the word is embedded and by visual features, such as length and silhouette of the word.

This stage and style of learning to read is much like learning to recognize *spoken* language. An infant develops growing recognition of repeated sound patterns—words, phrases—as they are associated with certain objects or activities in his environment, and at first his understanding of words and phrases is highly dependent on that context. For a while, he will not recognize the word when it is spoken elsewhere. Thus, a toddler who is learning to associate the word *toast* at the breakfast table with the browned crispy bread he is given will not so quickly recognize the word if it comes up in living room conversation. In our illustration of the word STOP, a child will recognize it on a red, octagonal street sign before he is able to recognize it in isolation or in another context. For this reason, children who can read their storybooks at home may recognize many words in the context of that particular book, but not elsewhere.

Stage II Reading—Phonic Analysis and Synthesis

Reading shifts to the Stage II process, requiring more analysis, when the demand for distinguishing between words is too great to be managed by holistic recognition. For example, the two words *money* and *monkey* are similar in many ways, but they probably could be distinguished by a child reading only holistically because of silhouette. The 'k' that rises up in the middle of monkey is the sort of distinctive visual feature that assists in sorting out the perception of two words, even when one is unaware of /k/ as a specific sound element in the word. On the other hand, the two words *horse* and *house* have identical silhouettes, and it is only by looking closely and taking account of the sound values of the letters that one knows which is which. The words *casual* and *causal* offer an example of even greater similarity in appearance, where even a fluent adult reader has to slow down and look carefully.

Stage II reading involves analyzing the phonic elements of a word, combining them in the proper order, and then synthesizing the component sounds into a recognizable word. In this process, the visual image of the word does not carry with it a meaning, a concept. The word rather appears as a string of letters whose message, or meaning, has not yet been decoded. I have made up a word—s e n t i n a s c u l a t e—which *you* must decode because its image carries no previously established concept for you. If you were given a meaning for it and a few more opportunities to encounter and decode the word anew, you would learn it and soon recognize it so quickly that you would be unaware of decoding it. At that point you would be reading the word at a Stage III level.

We'll stay with Stage II a while longer. Keep in mind that at this stage the child switches from a process that is almost totally visual—the total image STOP *meant* something—to a process in which visual symbols (the graphemes) must be converted into sounds that are strung together to make a recognizable *heard word* that has meaning. The sounds of individual letters have no meaning—they are abstract bits, building blocks, that will lead to a meaningful concept if they are tracked, sounded out, and assembled correctly.

Progression of Reading Stages I–III

It is a fascinating aspect of the progression from Stage I to Stage II that it mirrors the historical development of written language. That is, the sequence of stages that children traverse in learning to read repeats the stages that early man passed through in creating a writing system. The first written languages were pictures: Egyptian hieroglyphics, Indian pictograms, and Chinese symbols, which date back, we believe, to the fourth millennium B.C. Like a STOP sign read with Stage I competence, the picture represented a concept, an idea. Alphabetic languages appear to have developed one to two thousand years later, as people, initially the Phoenicians, came to see that it would be far more efficient and useful to have a graphic writing system that represented the component sounds of a word rather than the concept. Because there is a finite, and relatively small, number of sound elements in any language, it is far simpler to represent words graphically by writing out the symbols of the sound elements, rather than by inventing a new symbol for every language concept. The Chinese have only recently begun to convert to an alphabet system, some six thousand years after they developed pictorial symbols. It is reported that Mao realized in the 1930s that if the language remained one of pictorial characters representing concepts, which had to be learned one by one, the Chinese could never hope to overcome illiteracy.

In alphabetic languages, there are a great number of items and processes that must be learned in order to analyze a word. This process of analysis is the most specific meaning of the term *decoding*. It implies that the child is figuring out, or analyzing, in order to read, rather than reading by holistic word recognition. As a rule of thumb, normal readers will learn all of these elements by the end of second grade, at least to the level of mastery, and many will have achieved automaticity as well (Snow, Burns, & Griffin, 1998; Foorman, Francis, & Fletcher, 1997). Most of the elements are facts that must be committed to memory as *paired associates*—that is, as two things that go together. In reading, the majority of paired associates to be learned are the linkings of grapheme and phoneme, often referred to as *symbol-sound correspondence* or *spelling-to-sound correspondence*. In other words, the child must be able to traverse back and forth with relative ease between the graphic symbol and the sound it represents.

Let's go back to the word "cat" for a moment. When the child *sees* the word 'cat' and its initial letter, the auditory image of the phoneme 'cuh' must come to mind. Conversely, when the child *hears* the word "cat" and wants to write it, he has to isolate the sound (or phoneme) of the initial consonant in order to bring to mind the graphic image of the letter 'c.' For a while, children struggle with calling up the correct paired associate. To become proficient to the point of automaticity they need many experiences in

> *looking,* and recalling to mind the paired sound (or auditory image); and
>
> *hearing,* and recalling to mind the paired symbol (or graphic image).

The process involves the mental activities of perception, memory, and imaging. Normal beginning readers are able to carry out these activities to the point of automaticity, although there is wide variation in how quickly they achieve mastery and then automaticity.

(This is roughly the same mental activity that takes place when you see a familiar face and try to remember the name of that person, or hear someone's name and try to visualize the person. Usually, if the person involved is someone you know well, the name and the visual image are so intimately associated as to seem to be one thing, not two. If you have to struggle to attach a name to a face, you may better understand the plight of children who do not achieve automaticity in connecting a written symbol with the sound it represents.)

Sally, a very intelligent, hardworking, 7½-year-old second grader whom we will be discussing at greater length in Chapter 6, offers a fine example of difficulties with mastery and automaticity in her response to the grapheme 'ch.' She had learned the sound that 'ch' makes, and when it appeared in a familiar word such as child *or* chair, *she read it correctly, pronouncing the phoneme /ch/. When it appeared in an unfamiliar word, she sometimes sounded it out correctly, but at other times she would respond to the letters 'c' and 'h' as with their separate, discrete sounds /c/ and /h/. For the most part, she would correct herself, indicating that she had achieved some degree of mastery of this phonic element, but was far from automaticity.*

Sally demonstrates cognizance, and some mastery. James, on the other hand, illustrates lack of cognizance of the sound /ch/. At age 12, with normal intelligence, he was found to be unable to read when he entered a new special education program. When tested for phonics knowledge, he could not say what sound 'ch' made, even though he lived on Peachum Street, and could write his address correctly. Thus, although he uttered the /ch/ sound, and included its grapheme 'ch' in his writing of a familiar word, he had no awareness (or cognizance) of the sound as a specific, isolated entity.

Stage III Reading—Mature Reading

We move now to Stage III reading, or mature reading. It appears similar to Stage I reading, and for the experienced reader, it feels more like Stage I reading as well because there is little sense of decoding, of actually sounding out a word. A fast look reveals the identity of the whole word; the concept for which it stands springs instantly to mind. In fact, however, there is an increasingly thorough and deep awareness of the elements that compose the word, but there is no need to stop and sound out letters or syllables.

Stage III reading is not a monolithic competency arrived at one day, which then works on any and all reading material encountered. As children become more familiar with certain words, and with the syllables that appear frequently in our language (such as 'ing,' 'est,' and 'tion'), they move into reading with greater fluency and accuracy, with a Stage III awareness. That is, they recognize the word on sight, but can analyze it if necessary. Most young readers in grades one through three are reading with some combination of Stages I, II, and III approaches. The older and more experienced they get, the greater the proportion of reading they carry out at Stage III. Normal readers vary widely in the pace of their progress through the developmental stages of reading, just as they vary in achieving automaticity. The job is considered essentially complete when they are able to read almost all words in their speaking vocabulary at a Stage III level.

No one ever graduates entirely out of Stages I and II. Even addicted readers come across words they cannot decode and must regress to a Stage I kind of reading. One example is reading Russian novels. The names of the characters are often too unfamiliar for us to read accurately, particularly if they include combinations of letters that don't occur in English and therefore preclude a good Stage II phonemic analysis. Thus, we recognize a character in the novel as the one with the long name that begins with 'm'; if there are two long-named characters whose names begin with 'm,' we use some additional features to differentiate—the one with the two 'g's in the middle versus the one with the 'y' at the end, perhaps. We can read a thousand pages and know the characters intimately without knowing how to pronounce their names. This is another form of Stage I reading, in which the visual symbol is associated directly with the concept, never passing through the middle stage of phonemic analysis and often never pronounced. (Many people, following their habits of inner voice accompaniment to silent reading, will develop some vague auditory image of the name, which may or may not resemble the correct pronunciation.)

Perhaps more common in everyday life is the regression to Stage II reading when one comes across an unfamiliar but decipherable term—such as *sentinasculate*—or new proper nouns that appear in the newspaper, such as Bhopal, Chernobyl, Lockerbie. If we find them first in print, rather than hearing them on TV, we notice them as unfamiliar and then work at deciphering them according to our best guess about phonemic values and accent. We may make minor errors, but we will correct these when we hear someone pronounce the word on TV. We'll then know it's Lockerbee and not Lockerbye. Russian novels and unfamiliar place-names are examples of the moments when reading demands special attention, when it calls for conscious, thoughtful processing rather than the automatic processing that usually carries the mature reader along very well. It is analogous to driving under difficult road conditions.

Stage III or mature reading can continue to develop, extending one's capacity to take in larger quantities of text rapidly. How far this develops depends on how skilled the reader has become in this sort of automatic information processing and how familiar is the material he reads. Thus, we quickly scan and recognize "Once upon a time" at the beginning of a fairy tale. Professional literature with redundant vocabulary and phraseology also lends itself to quick decoding. At this level, it is clear that prior knowledge, vocabulary, and conceptual understanding, which are the stuff of reading comprehension, contribute greatly to the speed and efficiency with which we process the printed word. In addition, the state of our inner language development, and the quickness with which past language experience comes to mind and interacts efficiently with the written text, affect how quickly we recognize text.

Differentiating between Reading Stages

Because Stage I and Stage III reading performance in some ways resemble each other, we may misinterpret children's reading competence. When we hear children read aloud we may find it difficult or impossible to know whether they are knowledgeable and competent regarding the code or are recognizing whole words in a global fashion. In both cases, they recognize words as wholes, without phoneme-by-phoneme sounding out. Children who read well with largely Stage I competency do so by other means, such as good whole word recognition, use of context and pictures, familiarity with the content, and strong language experience. For this reason a number of children who are found to be poor readers in the later grades have escaped detection in the early grades.

Difficulty in differentiating between Stage I and Stage III understanding is not confined to reading acquisition. In an early version of a widely used individual intelligence test, this question appeared: "In what way are a nickel and a dime alike?" Children with Stage I or Stage III understanding generally answered, "They're both money." Stage III understanding in this instance includes knowledge about the monetary values of each coin, as well as the fact that both are subsumed under the term *money*. Stage I understanding is vague and global, without knowledge of the specific and relative values of the coins. Stage II understanding focuses on the details and lacks conceptual integration; children at this level tend to get stuck on how the two coins are different, and while usually familiar with the general concept "money," fail to mention it because they are preoccupied with Stage II detail. Thus, we have the paradoxical situation of children at a relatively more advanced stage of understanding failing an item for which the less advanced receive full credit.

We all move through the three stages during the course of our lives, as we come across new and unfamiliar things and ideas. We learn about their particulars and then understand them in a more integrated way, not only in relation to themselves but in relation to other aspects of our learning over the years. However, this does not hold true with the phonic code of our language, unless one specializes in some aspect of linguistics and learns more about the history and underlying connections associated with various aspects of written English. For the bulk of the population of normal readers, however, learning of the code is pretty much completed by the end of second grade. Some more sophisticated aspects are added later on, such as the rule for when the letter 'c' is sounded as /s/ and when as /k/.

BASIC READING COMPETENCIES

Up to this point, we have been discussing reading acquisition from the perspective of naturally occurring developmental patterns that provide a framework for the information and competencies required in learning to read. The remainder of this chapter presents an overview of the basic competencies that underlie reading ability. There is no single, agreed-upon list of competencies, although there is general agreement among reading researchers. Researchers sometimes refer to the "lumpers" and "splitters" among them. Lumpers deal with relatively large clusters of items, emphasizing what they have in common, while splitters aim to make fine discriminations, and establish more individual categories that highlight differences. In discussing the reading process we lean toward lumping, and focus mainly on those competencies, the absence or weakness of which are most likely to contribute significantly to impaired reading acquisition.

In this discussion, two important technical terms are *phonology* and *orthography*. Phonology refers to the *sound* of units of language, and orthography refers to the *appearance* of units of language. Phonology thus is an abstract noun that embraces phonemes and larger units of spoken language; orthography refers to graphemes and larger units of written language. Competencies in perceiving and recalling phonological and orthographic units, small and large, are key elements in reading acquisition.

The competencies required for reading have little to do with intelligence. It is true that a number of precocious children, usually of very high intelligence, teach themselves to read even before entering school, but so far as acquiring reading through standard elementary school instruction is concerned, there is little correlation between the ease and speed of learning to read and intelligence test scores (Lyon & Chhabra, 1996; Siegel, 1989). Research shows a consistently stronger correlation between reading skill and what are sometimes referred to as *modular systems,* following a concept of Fodor (1983). Modular systems, in this context, are mental processes that function with speed, automaticity, and autonomy. They are autonomous in the sense that they are independent of general conceptual intelligence and knowledge base; their functioning does not depend on how well or poorly central intellectual processes operate. This explains why many retarded children can learn to read, while many very intelligent children have difficulty with reading. The prominent modular systems involved in reading acquisition, in both visual and auditory modes, are memory, perception, and discrimination.

Here we present the competencies for reading roughly in order of Werner's three stages. Using the framework can, through repetition, strengthen understanding of the stages themselves, and at the same time make the competencies discussed easier to grasp.

Stage I

Stage I reading, the stage of whole word recognition without knowledge of phonemes and the alphabetic principle, depends on visual memory for the printed word—that is, orthographic memory. The look of the word at this stage may include its context, such as with the red STOP sign. Or it may be a word that is so familiar that it will stand out in a less specific or colorful context, such as one's own name. It may be a word that is recognized with the help of other cues, such as a picture on the page. In a strict sense, though, we would not consider it as a word identified from its own orthography until it can be recognized when it stands alone. To accomplish this, the child must be able to establish an orthographic representation of the word—that is, a mental image of the appearance of the word. The mental image must be strong enough so that when the word is seen again, it will resonate with the "template" that has been established from prior exposures to the word. Teachers refer to words learned and read in this fashion as *sight words* or *look-say words*.

The most significant aspect of Stage I reading is that it is almost entirely a visual activity, requiring recognition of the shape of the whole word, along with some significant features that help distinguish it from words with a similar configuration. Sound is important in that there must be an automatic association between the look of the whole word, and the *sound* of the word represented; in other words, the visual image of the word must call to mind the matching auditory image. But phonological sensitivity and awareness of the presence and role of phonemes are not involved.

Stage II

Stage II reading depends very heavily on learning the code, on being able to work through a word, in a left-to-right direction, and finding the correct phoneme (sound) to match each letter or combination of letters (grapheme). Whereas understanding the alphabetic principle was not necessary at Stage I, it is now very important. Children come to understand that sounds are represented by letters. They learn the paired associations between graphemes and phonemes, learn to sound out words in correct sequence, and learn to blend the sounds into a recognizable word. They now inspect words more closely than before, in order to distinguish between look-alike words such as *house* and *horse, from* and *form, block* and *black.* They also become more aware of the presence and function of punctuation marks, particularly periods, commas, and question marks. In the course of this learning, it becomes apparent to the normal beginning reader that the sounds "map onto" the written letters in a very precise, sequential way, and that she must pay attention to all elements of the word.

An illustration of impaired ability to match sounds to spelling may be helpful here, because it is hard for skilled readers to imagine a difficulty of this sort.

> *Mr. Green, an intelligent, successful businessman in his thirties came to me for an evaluation of his learning difficulties. The testing included a spelling test, and for the word* equipment *he wrote* eqpmen. *In going over his work with him, I ignored the missing vowels near the beginning of the word, and focused on the missing consonant at the end of the word, because it seemed an easier task to isolate and identify that clearly sounded*

/t/. I told him something was missing at the end of the word, pronounced the word again stressing the /t/ sound, and asked him if he could complete the word with the missing sound. He puzzled over that for a few moments, and then wrote eqpmenment.

In Mr. Green's case the problem may be greater than not matching sounds to spelling. He may not be sufficiently able to segment the word into its component sounds, a task that is generally performed by kindergarten children who, for example, might be asked to repeat the word *cowboy* and then say it again leaving off *cow*. They can get practice with other multi-syllabic words and eventually they will be able to segment words into their component phonemes—for example, by saying the word *smile* and then saying it again leaving off the /s/. Children can develop this awareness of separate phonemes even before they know letter names. By the time a child begins to learn the elements of Stage II reading, he must be able to use this skill. Most children are able to do so by early first grade.

Skills and Conceptual Understanding Underlying Stage II Reading

- Phonological awareness: the ability to segment the phonemes and syllables within a word.
- Understanding of the alphabetic principle.
- Memory for sound-symbol paired associates.
- Attention to visual detail in discriminating among look-alike letters (*black* and *block, big* and *pig*) and noting punctuation signs.
- Attention to sequence in discriminating among look-alike words (*from* and *form*).
- Auditory memory and ready access to a sufficient inner word bank (that is, vocabulary) to allow for blending decoded sounds (from grapheme to phoneme) into a recognizable word.
- Visual memory for recognition of whole words (carried over from Stage I).

Stage III

These competencies are the significant modular cognitive skills that enable the child to move along to Stage III reading. At this stage, he quickly recognizes familiar words at an automatic level and can decode unfamiliar words with minimal difficulty—as you decoded *sentinasculate* earlier in this chapter. Stage III reading requires no special skills, beyond those already acquired. Unless there is an impediment to mastering Stage I and II skills, it is generally only a matter of practice— of reading material at a level appropriate for age, grade, and level of vocabulary and conceptual understanding—to develop word identification skills to the level of automaticity.

Top-Down/Bottom-Up Interactivity

There is one more competency to mention in this discussion of normal reading acquisition, although it is far from being a modular skill. It is, on the contrary, quite complex in the number of cognitive skills it comprises. In the professional literature it is referred to as *top-down / bottom-up interactivity,* and it is of critical importance both to learning the code and to reading comprehension. Those who champion direct and thorough teaching of phonics have argued that much of reading acquisition takes place from the *bottom up*—that is, from the basic building blocks of phonemes and graphemes at the bottom, to the higher levels of meaning. A presumption in this point of view is that interest and motivation are more likely to develop if the child feels secure with the ability to recognize or sound out words and that competence in being able to decode the words on the page is also rewarding in and of itself.

Those who challenge this heavy phonics approach and promote a *top-down* method of instruction, often referred to in recent years as Whole Language, argue that the basic elements in reading acquisition are enjoyment of the content and the quest for meaning. They believe that instruction should begin with meaningful texts that engage the child's interest and are relevant to her life experience. Knowledge of the code is expected to develop naturally, in the same way that spoken language developed, and in the interim children will be able to read, aided by strong motivation and interest, some basic sight word recognition, some familiarity with the content, various context clues including pictures, and intelligent guessing. There is a presumption of universal, competent, linguistic development in this point of view, and the conviction that if provided a stimulating and supportive educational environment, all children will in time learn the code. The more commonly accepted position at this time is that reading acquisition occurs in both directions, interactively. For a time, some learners may lean more heavily on the code and others on more general, "whole" language elements. Among normally developing readers, the interaction between code and meaning elements do come together, with accuracy, fluency, good comprehension, and automaticity.

How quickly automaticity occurs is a matter of individual innate ability in the areas of competence required for reading, in combination with interest and the availability of appropriate reading material and adult support. We noted earlier how learning to read is like learning to drive a car, play a musical instrument, or use an athletic skill. The distribution of natural aptitudes in all these realms covers a broad spectrum, from highly talented and precocious, to clumsy, uncomprehending, and slow to learn. Some children are more apt and seem to understand concepts and pick up skills intuitively, in one or several areas, with little or no direct instruction. Others are not so quick, but they learn in good time and are competent enough to employ those skills for further learning and general development. Those with great difficulty in catching on to how to read the letters, or hold the violin bow, or keep themselves upright on a ski slope, are likely to avoid the activity if possible, and thus deprive themselves of the additional instruction and practice that would eventually make the task easier. The first of these, the weak readers, are the children who will concern us in the following chapters.

▶ 3

Dyslexia, a Learning Disability

Awareness of dyslexia began developing in the late nineteenth century, long before there was any recognition of other, analogous impairments of learning. Today, dyslexia is seen to be one of several types of *learning disability,* all of which share certain defining characteristics. In the first part of this chapter we will discuss several aspects of learning disabilities: defining characteristics, etiology, and a number of common misconceptions about them. In the second part we will take up matters that are specific to dyslexia and the reading process.

LEARNING DISABILITIES

Defining Characteristics of Learning Disabilities

- Underlying Neurological Basis
- Uneven Profile of Cognitive Abilities
- Interference with the Acquisition of Basic Academic Skills

Underlying Neurological Basis
The underlying neurological basis of learning disabilities is manifested in the inadequate functioning of cognitive operations related to learning, such as memory, perception, fine

motor coordination, and attention. These operations are dependent on various aspects of brain development, organization, and "circuitry." (Although many metaphors relating brains to computers are incorrect, the connections among brain structures and processes *is* roughly analogous to computer circuitry.) Inadequate functioning is determined by history, observations, and psychological testing of the basic cognitive operations related to learning.

There is no single test for learning disabilities. The diagnosis is made clinically, through induction, based on the data derived from history; from observations of the student as he speaks, reads, writes, spells, and so on; and from test scores. Learning disabilities can result from brain injury or disease, but they are far more prevalent among individuals with medically healthy brains.

Uneven Profile of Cognitive Abilities

The term *cognitive abilities* refers to the various and somewhat discrete skills that make up general intelligence. These skills include the modular systems such as perception, attention, and memory that become so thoroughly automatized that one is unaware, or scarcely aware, of the ongoing activity. Learning disabilities result from an imbalance among cognitive abilities, especially the modular skills, resulting in a very uneven profile of abilities when test results are plotted on a graph. While the profiles of most people fluctuate mildly in a generally narrow plane, those of the learning disabled show significant peaks and valleys. For example, a common profile for dyslexia is one in which scores on tasks requiring conceptual understanding are well above average, while scores on tasks requiring memory for rote information are much lower.

Interference with the Acquisition of Basic Academic Skills

This criterion for learning disability is not so much scientific as it is practical. There are many people who meet the two criteria above—neurological basis and uneven cognitive profile—but who do not experience academic difficulties. For example, people who are tone-deaf have a neurologically based difficulty, and an uneven profile of cognitive abilities in which the ability to perceive, remember, and produce tonal pitches is very low, yet tone-deaf individuals are not generally considered learning disabled, because this "disability" doesn't affect academic success. In addition, there are many individuals who test poorly on some of the underlying, specific skills most frequently associated with learning disabilities, but whose academic abilities appear to be unimpaired. In many cases they have found ways to compensate for specific weaknesses, and they are often successful because they don't have weaknesses in other realms (social, emotional, or intellectual) that sap their spirit and motivational energy.

Over the years, the term *learning disability* has become limited to those learning difficulties that have an underlying neurological base. Difficulties in learning that stem from other biological factors such as mental retardation, or from emotional impediments or environmental circumstances, do not warrant the designation of "learning disability," although an individual may have *both* a learning disability and other kinds of learning difficulties.

The Etiology of Learning Disabilities

Although neuroscience cannot yet explain the cause of specific weakened functions, there is a long-standing, broad categorization of etiologic factors that provides a perspective and a framework for this large and mixed bag of mild to severe dysfunctions (Cattell, 1950). There are four categories, and as they progress from the first to the last they become broader, with each category encompassing those that came before.

Genetic

Many of those with learning disabilities have inherited them through genes transmitted from their parents. In some cases a parent has or had a learning disability, although this may not become apparent until the parent is interviewed about his or her child; then it suddenly comes to mind that the parent suffered similar difficulties with learning, usually in the elementary grades. Sometimes, neither parent has any sign of learning disability, but there are members of the extended family who have. Among those with dyslexia, research indicates that at least 50 percent of the cases are hereditary (Pennington, 1991).

Innate

Together with the first group who have inherited a disability through direct genetic transmission, this category includes those who, during the gestational period, have undergone some genetic or chromosomal mutation that creates learning disabilities. We cannot yet scientifically detect these mutations, but we do know of at least two syndromes caused by chromosomal abnormality—Turner's and Klinefelter's—which carry with them learning disability profiles. Girls with Turner's syndrome (one X chromosome but no second sex-determining chromosome) tend to have poor visual-perceptual, visual-spatial, and visual-motor abilities. Boys with Klinefelter's syndrome (an extra X chromosome) are more prone to language disabilities.

Congenital

This category includes all those etiologic factors from conception to birth. In addition to the previous two categories related to genetic composition, it takes in all of the pregnancy and birth factors that may result in cognitive dysfunction. These include prematurity, anoxia, bleeding, alcohol, drugs, X ray, faulty diet, German measles and other infections, and difficult labor. An early study by Kawi and Pasamanick (1959) reviewed the hospital birth records of 205 boys with reading disorders, and records of 205 control subjects without reading disorders. Of the boys with reading disorders, 16.6 percent had been exposed to two or more maternal complications, most of them leading to fetal anoxia (insufficient supply of oxygen to the fetus), as compared with 1.5 percent of the control group. More recent research has concentrated on specific causative agents. For example, Streissguth (1986) cited the effects of smoking and drinking during pregnancy, and Sever (1986) has reviewed the ill effects of maternal infection during the gestational period.

Constitutional
This category covers all of the biological factors that can cause cognitive dysfunction, adding postnatal events such as head injury, meningitis, encephalitis, ingestion of poisons such as lead paint, and malnutrition due to the foregoing pre- and paranatal events.

Facts and Fictions about Learning Disabilities
The Evolving Definition of Learning Disabilities
Misconceptions about learning disabilities abound among the public, including many educators and mental health professionals. Many of these erroneous beliefs stem from confusing terminology and from obsolete formulations and definitions that were put forth as the field was developing. The term *learning disability* itself was coined only in 1963 by Samuel Kirk, one of the earliest pioneers in this field (Kirk, 1963). Kirk was the leading author of The Illinois Test of Psycholinguistic Abilities (ITPA), one of the first psychological tests designed specifically to identify the learning disabled. The ITPA was first published in 1968, and although it has been largely abandoned in the wake of greater understanding and revised theories about learning disabilities, we owe Dr. Kirk a great debt. Until 1963, the learning disabled, if they were identified at all, were viewed as part of a larger set of children manifesting learning problems and some behavior problems that could not be attributed to either mental retardation or emotional disturbance. In the 1940s and 1950s, such children were referred to as "organic," meaning their difficulties were assumed to result from brain damage, although no frank brain disease or injury was apparent. Later the term became *minimal brain damage* and then *minimal brain dysfunction* came along, in recognition of the fact that there was no apparent brain *damage,* minimal or otherwise. Hyperactive children

and those prone to "tuning out" also fell within these diagnostic categories, whether or not they had learning difficulties. Kirk succeeded in splitting off the learning disabled from this general pool and put the spotlight on their uneven profiles of cognitive skills, which remain the *sine qua non* of learning disabilities to this day.

Once the term *learning disabilities* entered the professional literature, there followed years—decades actually—of serious effort to define the term. For many years, the reigning definition was one of exclusion: If a child had difficulty in one or more of the processes of speech, language, reading, spelling, writing, or arithmetic, and was of at least average intelligence, with no sensory or motor handicap, or emotional disturbance, or cultural or instructional disadvantage, he was then determined to be learning disabled.

Misconception #1: All Learning Disabled Are of Average or Above-Average Intelligence

This brings us to the first major misconception about learning disabilities, the belief that the learning disabled are, by definition, of average or better intelligence, and have no other impediments to learning. This is an illogical position. Given the various ways in which one can become learning disabled, there is no reason to think that only the otherwise sound, healthy, and competent can be learning disabled. The less intelligent, the emotionally disturbed, the physically handicapped are also vulnerable to the effects of birth trauma, poor nutrition, genetic mutation, or hereditary predisposition. It is understandable that in the early days of trying to define learning disabilities, it seemed necessary to rule out of the definition any other handicapping condition that critics could claim to be the cause of learning deficit. Pioneers in this field wanted to be in the position of saying, "Look, this child is, with the exception of reading (or arithmetic or writing, and so on) fine and able in all other respects. Therefore the problem is something else, and the something else is learning disability." Today there is recognition among researchers and many clinicians in the field that good intelligence is not a criterion for establishing the presence of learning disability. Unfortunately, because this fact is not widely recognized among the public, many learning disabled children who score below average on intelligence testing, but are capable of learning, fail to receive appropriate remedial education.

The learning disabilities of emotionally disturbed children are also often missed, but for different reasons. Some of them are so concerned about appearing stupid that they make a great fuss when faced with difficult schoolwork, preferring to have their teachers and parents think of them as unwilling rather than unable to do their work. Harold, 13 years old, had an unusual and very severe problem with spelling that made him unable to write anything he could be proud of. When it came time to write he would wail and cry, leave the classroom, and carry on like a 3-year-old having a tantrum. His teachers saw his being overwrought and uncooperative as part of his immaturity and had no idea that although his reading was at sixth-grade level, he was truly unable to spell as well as the average first grader.

Misconception #2: Learning Disabilities Are Present-or-Absent Conditions

Another misconception about learning disabilities is the belief that they are present-or-absent conditions, like measles or pregnancy. This is not the case. The cognitive weaknesses that underlie learning disabilities extend over a continuum from mild to severe. At the mild end, these weaknesses shade into the normal range, where they can be conceptualized as being within the average span of individual differences. The mildness or severity of one's learning disability depends on how many different cognitive processes are affected and how severe the deficits are in each.

Misconception #3: Many More Males Than Females Have Learning Disabilities

It is very natural for people to assume that among the learning disabled, boys greatly outnumber girls, because there are far more learning disabled boys than girls in special education classes. A U.S. Department of Education report noted that the percentages of learning disabled boys and girls in the schools were 72 and 28, respectively (Lerner, 1993). However, when learning disabled children are identified in research settings rather than school and clinic settings, the difference between the numbers of boys and girls is much smaller, sometimes approaching equality (Snow, Burns, & Griffin, 1998). There is a strong consensus among researchers that boys are more heavily represented among children referred for special education because they are more disruptive in regular classrooms than girls (Anderson, 1997). It is not just that girls are less frequently discipline problems who make it hard for the teacher to conduct class. Because girls are, as a group, more compliant and interested in pleasing the teacher, they are more likely to get help on their assignments from parents and peers, thus masking their learning difficulties for a number of years. Eileen, whose case is presented in Chapter 6, is an example of such a girl.

Misconception #4: Learning Disabilities Can Be "Cured"

With appropriate assistance, children can be helped to overcome some aspects of their learning disabilities, but in general, underlying weaknesses in competencies such as attention, memory, perception, and language fluency remain. For example, children with dyslexia frequently become accurate and comfortable readers, but they often have continuing difficulty in such areas as reading speed, spelling, and foreign language learning. Additional instruction and extensive practice can help them achieve greater mastery in these areas as well, but the slow pace of learning and the need for greater than average amounts of practice usually remain.

Misconception #5: "Developmental" Problems Are Outgrown with the Passage of Time

Confusion has been created through dual meanings of the term "developmental." In the medical sense, learning disabilities are labeled *developmental* when they are seen as a condition present since birth or very soon after, and therefore as a built-in attribute of the person's constitution, although observable signs or symptoms of the learning disability might come to light only years later. The term "developmental" distinguishes a condition from one that is *acquired* later in life through accident or disease. For example, the children we see with dyslexia almost always have developmental dyslexia. Adults with acquired dyslexia have suffered some trauma to the brain that has damaged or destroyed some part of the process of normal, skilled reading. Stroke, gunshot wounds, brain tumors, and head injury are among the causes of acquired dyslexia.

Teachers are more familiar with the term in contexts such as *developmental lag* or *developmental delay,* which carry the notion that something may be slow in developing but will come along on its own in good time. Because of the strong trend in educational settings to think of development as a healthy and natural process that needs to be respected and supported rather than intruded on, many teachers assume that a developmental problem is one that will straighten itself out or "catch up" in the course of time. They often express this meaning of the term when they ask about a student's learning difficulty: "Is it a problem we need to do something about, or is it 'just' developmental?" In the case of dyslexia, the problem is likely to be developmental in both meanings of that term: a constitutional "given," and also a lag in learning. But as will be discussed extensively in later chapters, the fact that a student has an inborn limitation on the rate of development of reading skills does not make intervention unwarranted.

To date there is no clear-cut, fully agreed-upon definition of learning disabilities. Two frequently cited definitions are found in Appendix A. The earlier one was formulated in 1968; in 1975 it was used to define the term in Public Law 94-142, the first comprehensive federal legislation for special education. The later one was proposed in 1988 by the National Joint Committee on Learning Disabilities (NJCLD), a professional organization that includes representatives from the fields of speech and language, reading, dyslexia, and learning disabilities. This definition is generally seen as an improvement on the earlier one, clarifying that learning disabilities can coexist with other handicapping conditions and may occur over the life span. Nevertheless, both definitions are vague and open to multiple interpretations by clinicians and researchers (Lyon, 1996).

DYSLEXIA

Dyslexia, the most widely known of the learning disabilities, was first brought to public notice in 1896, when an ophthalmologist named Morgan published an article entitled "A Case of Congenital Word-Blindness" in the *British Medical Journal* (Morgan, 1896). Only twenty-one years later did the next significant publication appear, also by an ophthalmologist, J. Hinshelwood (1917), who wrote a monograph on the subject, describing many cases of otherwise healthy children who could not read, and continuing to call it congenital word-blindness. He emphasized two facts—that there were often several cases from the same family, and that the symptoms were very close to those of adults who had lost the ability to read because of injury to the brain. From this, Hinshelwood hypothesized an inherited brain defect.

Samuel T. Orton* was also a physician, but his training and experience were in neurology, neuropathology, and psychiatry. In 1924, in his role as head of the department of psychiatry in the medical school of the State University of Iowa in Iowa City, and also as the founding director of the state mental hospital in Iowa City, he recommended using mobile psychiatric units to serve the mental hygiene needs of the people of Iowa. He was soon invited by the doctors, welfare agencies, and school authorities of Greene County, Iowa, to conduct a clinic there. When a 16-year-old boy was referred from a rural school be-

---

*The biographical information on Samuel Orton comes largely from Marcia Henry's work (Henry, 1998).

cause "he seemed bright but couldn't learn to read," Orton's previous experience in neuropathology with adults who had *acquired* word-blindness made him especially interested in the boy, whom he arranged to study at length in the hospital.

The county clinic soon found other pupils whose learning was impeded by reading difficulty, and Orton then had a pool of subjects whom he could study in some detail. He had profound insights into the nature of the disability and was exceptional both in his scientific method and acumen, and in his humanitarian outlook. He concluded that the problem did not involve a defective brain, but rather a maturational deviation in language development that lent itself to remedial training and offered a favorable prognosis. He dropped the term congenital word-blindness in favor of *developmental alexia*; that was later amended to *developmental dyslexia*, a more exact term meaning faulty reading rather than the lack of capacity to read.

What Orton learned in those years was transmitted to associates and students who worked with him in therapeutic and research settings, so that his work was carried on after his death in 1948. However, there was no general recognition of reading disability until a number of years after Kirk coined the term *learning disability* in 1963. In the interim Orton's followers did establish a few clinics that offered reading disabled children the systematic remedial program developed by Orton and his colleague Anna Gillingham. Dyslexia finally emerged as a recognized educational handicap affecting as much as 20 percent of the population if we include the mildest end of the spectrum. Another factor in the eventual spread of understanding of dyslexia was the founding of the Orton Society (later renamed The Orton Dyslexia Society, and most recently the International Dyslexia Association) by a group of his former associates in 1949.

As discussed in Chapter 1, the International Dyslexia Association, the major professional organization supporting research, training, and service in dyslexia, currently offers two official definitions of dyslexia (see Appendix A). There are two definitions because the researchers connected with the

organization want to limit the term to problems of word identification, while the training and service professionals prefer a
broader definition that will also include problems in reading
comprehension and other language problems. Time, usage,
and further research will eventually settle the question of definition. In the meantime, as noted earlier, in *this* book the term
dyslexia always refers to problems with word identification, in
either whole word recognition or decoding by phonemes.

There are some cases of comprehension difficulty that are
the *result* of a decoding or word recognition problem (Lyon &
Alexander, 1996/1997; Shankweiler, 1999). Such comprehension problems are more frequent among younger children, who
are skilled in neither whole word recognition nor the decoding
process; these children put so much effort into guessing at
words and sounds that they have little attention left to devote
to the content. It is similar to an automobile driver's experience in very bad road conditions. He has to concentrate so hard
on seeing through the fog, or controlling the speed, or being
careful not to hit the brakes too hard, that he can't attend to a
conversation with a passenger.

To recapitulate what we have established thus far about
dyslexia:

- It is a neurologically based condition that makes it difficult
  to identify the written word, due to weakness in one or
  more of the cognitive skills required for word identification.
- It is not correlated with intelligence, or any specific mental or emotional characteristic.
- It is on a continuum, ranging from mild to severe, depend-
  ing on how many decoding-related cognitive skills have
  been affected and how heavily affected each one is.

Specific Skill Weaknesses and Their Effects on Word Identification

Although there is extensive literature on dyslexia, much of it
based on long clinical experience and careful research, there is
no firm agreement on how to categorize the cognitive skills involved in reading, or how to rank the significance and fre-

quency of specific deficits. Nevertheless, there is general consensus as to what is involved in reading acquisition, even though individuals and working groups produce varying categories and lists of the skills and processes involved. In this as in other fields, there are "lumpers" and "splitters," those who conceptualize in large groupings and those who prefer to focus on small distinctions. Many of the differences among researchers and clinicians are the result of ongoing lumping and splitting, adding and eliminating, in a field that is still developing, albeit with increasing speed and success in recent years.

Let's look again at the list from Chapter 2 of cognitive skills involved in learning to read. Leaving out "understanding of the alphabetic principle" for the moment, the rest of the list can be seen to fall into two broad categories: perception and memory. Each of these two categories can be further divided into two subcategories, as seen below. The letters *A* and *V* in parentheses denote the skill as being auditory or visual.

PERCEPTION	*MEMORY*
Awareness	**Recognition**
Phonological (A)	Whole words (V)
Print (V)	Identify whole words from blended letters (A)
Discrimination	**Recall**
Look-alike letters and words (V)	Paired associates (A+V)
Sound-alike letters and words (A)	

For review and clarification, here are brief descriptions of each skill and a case example in which that skill is weak or lacking:

Phonological Awareness
The learner can discern sound segments within a spoken word, moving progressively from large elements, such as the small

words in compound words like *beanbag* or *snowplow*, to very small elements, such as the /t/ between the /s/ and /r/ in *struck*.

> *Hal, a 15-year-old boy with good reading ability but poor speech and terrible spelling, could not identify the /s/ in simple words such as* sick *or* sad.

Print Awareness
The reader notices the presence of written symbols, particularly those that easily escape notice, such as word endings and small punctuation marks.

> *Tony, an eighth grader, often failed to notice word endings, such as 'ed' or the final 's,' taking in only the root word. He omitted the letters in parentheses in the following words:* powerfull(y), thrill(ing), unload(ing).

Discrimination of Look-Alike Letters and Words
The student can readily analyze the particular parts of words that are easily mistaken, such as the beginning of *when* and *then*, the middle of *black* and *block*.

> *Dyslexic children who have learned the code don't always analyze far enough into individual words. Robert read* population *as* popularity.

Discrimination of Sound-Alike Letters and Words
Some letters are similar in their sound qualities, and take longer to differentiate. Among these are the short vowel sounds of /e/ and /i/, and the consonants /m/ and /n/.

> *Kelly couldn't hear the difference between* pit *and* pet.

Visual Recognition of Whole Words
One recalls the "look" of a whole word, without making use of decoding skills.

> *Eileen could sound out just about any word she came across, but she might not remember a word she had*

just decoded if she came across it again two lines later. She would then start sounding it out all over again, a kind of "reinventing the wheel" each time.

We will present Eileen and discuss her case more fully in Chapter 6.

Auditory Recognition of Whole Words

When words are sounded out letter-by-letter or syllable-by-syllable, one can make the slight inferential leap required to connect the sound segments into a known word.

John sounded out the word pho-to-graph-y *but could not make the leap to* photography, *a familiar word in his spoken and listening vocabulary.*

Memory for Sound-Symbol Pairs

After a reasonable amount of exposure and practice, one can respond to a printed letter with its alphabet name or the sound it makes.

Jane could not identify the letter A *in isolation, after repeated practice, and in spite of the fact that it appears in her name, which she can write and spell aloud.*

Lumping and splitting the skills this way highlights a number of interesting things:

- Whole word recognition is a Stage I skill. The rest are Stage II skills, requiring analysis and attention to detail.
- These skills are discrete and can be taught through direct instruction and practice.
- These skills are relatively easy to assess, for it takes little time, effort, or sophistication to determine whether a child has them if you are looking specifically for them.
- A strong conceptual grasp of the alphabetic principle (that is, that letters represent the component sounds in words) can be expected to develop as these skills are mastered, if it was not previously in place.

The list does not include two other factors in reading that are more complex and integrated capabilities: automaticity and language competence. (Language competence refers to inherent capacities for fluent verbal expression and ready comprehension of the communications of others.) When deficient, these capabilities do not readily lend themselves to direct instruction but rather depend on life experience and the general practice that comes with it, including listening to stories, conversing, and reading itself. Reading simple material, even too-easy material, fosters both language competence and automaticity, so although children need some degree of increasing challenge as they move along in their learning, there is also a great deal to be gained by allowing them, and even encouraging them, to read at whatever level is comfortable.

This applies to reading disabled adults as well. At age 42, Mr. Russo came for an evaluation of his spelling and writing difficulties, because he wanted to finish a four-year college program upon his upcoming retirement from the fire department. When I asked if he read much, he said that he used to enjoy reading detective fiction, but had stopped when his sister-in-law told him he should be reading more intellectual books. He tried that, got bored after a few pages, and quit, but he also did not return to the detective fiction.

Normal Reading and the Dyslexia Spectrum

Reading specialists have long recognized that dyslexia occurs on a wide spectrum from very mild to very severe. Recently we have become aware that dyslexia is also continuous with normal reading ability, with no clear line of demarcation between normal and disabled reading. Rather, it is probably more accurate to picture a reading ability continuum in the shape of a normal bell-shaped curve that covers the full range—from reading that is severely disabled, to reading that is precociously acquired and quickly reaches a high level of accuracy and fluency. (See Figure 3-1)

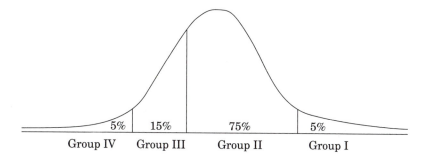

FIGURE 3-1

The research literature (Lyon, April, 1998) indicates that about 5 percent of children fall at each end of the reading continuum curve. Most children have mastered the major elements of reading by the end of second grade and can be thought of as falling in the middle section of the normal curve. The distribution of capabilities for learning to read means that we know in advance that some children will enter school each year already knowing how to read, most will enter not knowing how to read but able to learn to do so with regular school instruction, and some will experience difficulty and require more than the regular instructional program. Looking at the reading-dyslexia spectrum from a first-grade teacher's perspective, we can identify four groups of children arriving in their classrooms each year:

Group I
These are the precocious readers who have learned to read, often largely self-taught, before entering first grade. They are probably about 5 percent of the population.

Group II
This is the large majority of children, probably about 75 percent, who enter first grade with sufficient competencies to respond well to any standard reading instruction program that includes teaching of the phonics code. (According to various

studies [Lyon, 1997], only about 50 percent can be expected to learn relatively easily with formal instruction regardless of whether or not phonics is taught directly.)

Group III
These are children who do not learn to read easily, but who respond well to early intervention programs and remedial help. Often they have a reasonable understanding and some knowledge of basic reading skills, but have difficulty with speed or memory and can't progress at the pace of the larger group. They need more practice to gain mastery of what they understand before being asked to learn and remember new material. They make up about 15 percent of the entering children.

Group IV
These are the 5 percent of children who have more serious difficulties with learning to read, and who, if identified, would be diagnosed with moderate to severe dyslexia. They have significant weaknesses in some combination of the skills required for reading and generally require intensive remedial help.

We know that children with various levels of ability for reading will enter first grade, but we will not know for a while (and in some neglected cases "a while" has been years) which group each child belongs to. The most easily identifiable children are those in Group I, as their ability to read will be fully apparent if children are given even the most minimal screening when they arrive. Some children in Group IV may be recognized early as being *at risk* for learning to read because they have easily identifiable speech or language difficulties. However, not all children with speech and language difficulties have trouble learning to read; until formal reading instruction begins, one cannot be sure about children in this group either.

Once formal reading instruction begins, Group III and IV children will begin to have difficulty in some aspects of the program. Some will have trouble in recalling whole words (at the Stage I level); some will have trouble learning the elements of the code (Stage II skills). There will be those who have trouble with both, and they are likely to be the earliest who are identified by their teachers.

Failure to Identify Poor Readers

There are several reasons why many children who have difficulty mastering the code are not identified early in their school career. The most common one is that they are using other skills and information to make up for their lack of facility with the code. Many children who have trouble with the code have good sight word recognition, so they can recognize whole words and read them correctly without attending to the specific sounds of letters or letter groupings. (As described in Chapter 2, they are doing Stage I rather than Stage III reading.) If they also are able to make use of context clues, including the pictures that often accompany text, they may be quite successful in the early grades. Many of these children do learn a great deal of the code, but they are missing particular elements, which makes it impossible to decode the new, unfamiliar words they come across in more advanced reading material. Unless their reading skills are closely monitored, they can mislead their teachers for years and be seen as competent readers. By the later primary or middle school grades, when they are having difficulty doing their assignments and are in many cases having mild behavior problems, their lack of achievement is frequently attributed to psychological factors while reading weaknesses go undetected.

Tony, a boy of good intelligence in the eighth grade, was unable to sit with his homework for more than five minutes, and although he often did well on tests, he had five Fs on his last report card because of his failure to turn in assignments. Testing showed him to be reading about two years below grade level, while his math scores were two years above, at tenth-grade level. He couldn't decode the word freight *although he knew it wasn't* fright. *He misread many small words (it/in, that/than, a/the, when/with) and frequently dropped suffixes. His teachers had no idea that he was a poor reader, and understood his failure to turn in assignments solely as a behavior problem stemming from emotional problems (he had recently moved from another state to live with his father and stepmother).*

Other dyslexic children don't act out their troubles, but rather keep their worries to themselves. Their unhappiness and discomfort with reading are noted only at home if at all.

Carl, a fourth grader with an extremely high IQ, was not doing as well in reading as he was in all other subjects. His teachers were satisfied with his performance, but he was very unhappy with himself and asked to be moved from the middle to the lowest reading group. His parents sought psychiatric consultation, which in turn led to a request for testing. The testing revealed that he did not know the entire code—for example, the sound made by 'aw.' He could read saw *and* law, *which he recognized as sight words, but he could not read the nonsense word* taw. *(Note that if he is unable to read 'taw' he won't be able to decode unfamiliar words such as* Choctaw *or* tawny.*)*

Actually, it wasn't only that Carl didn't know the sound that 'aw' makes in our language. He wasn't aware of /aw/ as an element of the language. In the progression discussed in Chapter 2, *cognizance-mastery-automaticity*, Carl had not achieved the first stage, that of awareness of /aw/ as an entity to be studied and mastered. In his case, once it was pointed out to him he learned it quickly, and with sufficient practice it became automatic so that the correct sound for 'aw' came to mind immediately when he saw it in print.

Carl's not knowing 'aw' was significant not only as a gap in his knowledge of the code, but also as a "marker," an indicator that something was amiss in his linguistic processing. If, as a fourth grader of superior intelligence and high motivation to succeed, he hadn't noticed 'aw' as an element, it was likely that there were other things in the visual aspects of language processing that didn't work well for him. Sure enough, he made frequent errors in decoding because of reading too quickly. In many cases when he made a mistake, he could correct it when asked to go back and take another look. But like many young readers, he was trying to read aloud at a pace that didn't allow for sufficient visual analysis of the letters, and the sequence of letters, in each word. To put this another way, he was doing a lot of Stage I reading (global), which teachers may have assumed was Stage III reading (integrated), but was lacking in sufficient Stage II knowledge and skill (analytic).

Another common reason for the failure to identify dyslexic children is the widely held notion, applied in some instances to any and all weak readers, that these children are developing more slowly, and that if left to come along at their own pace they will eventually catch up. In many cases, when remedial help is offered, it is not sufficiently consistent or intensive. As a result, it is not uncommon to find children floundering in upper grades, still reading at very low levels.

> *Danny, a Group IV child, was not given any special attention until second grade. The remedial program then put in place was inadequate for the severity of his disability, and in the fourth grade he was still reading at first-grade level. After more than three years of inability to do regular schoolwork, he considered himself a total school failure. He had become a very anxious child, always expecting to do poorly, even in math, at which he excelled.*

At one time it was thought that dyslexia was a special kind of reading problem, a present-or-absent condition with characteristics different from the reading difficulties of other children who did not stand out as being particularly intelligent or highly verbal and therefore were not seen as "mysteriously" unable to read. We know now that those who have difficulty learning and using the phonics code are grappling with the same learning processes that everyone else does, and that what distinguishes them is that they have more difficulty in overcoming the sticking points along the way. To put it another way, they do not struggle to read, or experience failure, in some extraordinary fashion. They do not read backwards, although they do often mix up the sequence of letters.

The rest of us also mix up letters, albeit far less frequently and in circumstances where sequence is more easily misperceived. We misperceive words that look very much alike: *form* and *from*, *aboard* and *abroad*, *casual* and *causal*. And we misperceive and misremember when we drive by an unfamiliar street or highway sign too quickly, unable to catch and recall every letter in the proper order. We try to figure out what it might have said, and finally guess based on names of streets and towns that are familiar. The struggle of many dyslexic readers with book pages is not unlike our struggles with highway signs. Practice and experience lead to wider familiarity with words, for all of us on the highways and for dyslexics with their books.

Dyslexia is a highly treatable condition. It is continuing to plague students for two major reasons: one is the failure to identify it, and the other is the failure to provide appropriate classroom and individualized instruction to the children who need it. This is true for the mildest cases, including those children who don't merit an official diagnosis but who are weak in the requisite skills, as well as for the most severe cases.

▶ 4

Other Factors Influencing Learning

Children with weaknesses in the language, perception, and memory skills underlying reading will likely have trouble learning to read. And those with the most numerous and severe weaknesses generally will be the slowest to acquire good skills and face the greatest difficulty with overall school achievement. However, there are other factors that affect success or failure in learning. Among dyslexics, too, these other factors can have a major bearing on if, when, and how well they will learn to read.

Most outcomes in life are the result of multiple determinants, along with the effects of their interactions. Even though there is a tendency to look for the *single* cause of a particular problem, we know that life is usually more complicated than that. In this chapter we consider a number of the most common determinants that interfere with successful learning and, in combination with dyslexia, can turn a mild disability into a severe academic problem. The determinants are presented below according to the bio-social-psycho framework explicated by Erik Erikson (1963). The *biological factors* are generally present from birth; the *social factors* develop early from within the family and, sooner or later, from the wider community. The *psychological factors* are largely those that evolve into the personality of the individual, shaped in great measure by the interaction of the particular set of biological and social forces at work over the years.

BIOLOGICAL FACTORS

In addition to the specific functional weaknesses underlying dyslexia, there are other constitutional conditions that affect learning, although usually in a less direct, more generalized way. Most common and prominent among these are *temperament* and *attention*.

Temperament

Temperament is the broader category of the two. While it was once believed that infants are born with a *tabula rasa*, a clean slate upon which life circumstances determine the form and nature of their reactions to the world around them, it is now apparent that children enter the world with certain temperamental characteristics already in place. The fact that these qualities are biologically determined does not mean they are not subject to modification, but in the main, the aspects of temperament that are still present at school entry tend to be persistent.

Temperament has largely to do with an individual's response to stimulation, both external stimulation and the internal stimulation arising from thoughts, feelings, and bodily needs. Is the child easily excited, or does he have a high threshold for arousal? When excited, what is the nature and intensity of his response? Do physical needs (for food, elimination, and so forth) arise with some regularity and predictability? How readily can he adapt to new situations? What is the general level of his physical activity? How easily can the child be soothed? How adept is he at finding ways to soothe himself?

Most problems related to temperament can also be subsumed under the heading of weakness in self-regulation. As children grow they develop capacities to regulate, or modulate, their response patterns. They may need to become more aware and responsive, in some situations or in general; or they may need to filter out disturbing or distracting stimuli in order to retain their composure or concentration.

Sara had a fast response pattern. With school material that was relatively easy for her, her intuition and speed were very impressive. But when she came upon material that required a more patient, thoughtful approach, she failed to modify her response style and answered too quickly. Sometimes she would correct herself once she had given a wrong answer; apparently her mind had kept working on the problem even though her mouth or pencil had already spoken. At other times she moved on quickly to the next item.

Another aspect of temperament is mood. Many individuals appear to have an overriding emotional tone that colors response patterns; people are thus characterized as sunny, irritable, worried, or sad. Of course, life circumstances play a great role in promoting an established mood or a dominant style of behavioral response, and it is hard if not impossible to sort out origins according to nature versus nurture. Nevertheless, we don't want to lose sight of the fact that biology plays a large role in the temperamental makeup of some individuals. And while temperamental factors do not in themselves cause dyslexia, they can make it difficult for a child experiencing even mild dyslexic problems to handle frustration or put forth the extra effort required to strengthen weak skills.

Attention

Attention is a cognitive function that, in the past fifteen years or so, has received widespread notice in medical, psychiatric, and educational settings. Attention problems are frequently diagnosed as attention deficit disorder (ADD) or attention deficit/hyperactivity disorder (ADHD). Considerable confusion exists in the professional community as well as among the public as to the exact nature, etiology, and symptomatology of attention deficit. It is clear, however, that attention is one of the cognitive capacities, similar to those that directly underlie reading, that occur in the population across a wide spectrum, with some individuals showing unusual ability to attend, while others have notable difficulty.

One reason for confusion in discussing attention deficit disorders is the general failure to distinguish among various kinds of attention. The clearest delineation of the various forms of attention and how they are deployed in cognitive tasks has come from studying adults who *acquired* deficits as a result of head injury or brain disease. Once again, the study of unambiguous, acquired pathology has led to a better understanding of the *developmental* difficulties of children born with healthy, nondamaged brains but who experience a relative weakness in a particular cognitive function.

Four Forms of Attention

Four forms of attention have a strong effect on learning in general, and to some degree on learning to read in particular.

Selective attention has to do with perceiving and then directing one's attention to a particular task, while simultaneously screening out competing thoughts or external stimuli. The task might be as large and general as listening to the teacher's instructions or to a lecture, or as narrow and specific as watching for punctuation marks in a text.

Sustained attention is the ability to remain engaged with an activity over time, rather than turning away to follow another line of thought or engage in another activity. So, once a student has focused in on the teacher giving instruction, she then has to keep her attention there. And once she has started a phonics lesson with her tutor, she has to persist in giving it her attention. As a rule, it's easier to do that with a tutor than in a classroom, because the tutor will remain engaged with the student, adding his own sustained attention to the environment and helping the student redirect her attention when necessary.

Divided attention stands in sharp contrast to both selective and sustained attention, but often works cooperatively with them. Divided attention involves the distribution of attention so that we can attend to two or more things at once, usually one thing requiring more or lengthier attention, and the other relatively minor. An example of divided attention was discussed in Chapter 2 regarding driving: in routine traffic we can devote a minimal amount of conscious attention to the road (supplemented of course by automatic processing), while attending more intensely to conversation, radio broadcasts, or other thoughts. In a classroom, a youngster trying to pay strict attention to the teacher might find her seatmate trying to whisper something to her. If she decides to remain attentive to the teacher, she will have to give some brief period of attention to handling the momentary distraction. A child with weak capacities for divided attention might have trouble attending to accurate decoding while trying to follow the content, thus making reading errors. Another child might have the opposite difficulty, which is often harder to detect: that of concentrating so heavily on effortful decoding that he cannot simultaneously attend to the content.

Working memory is sometimes categorized as an aspect of memory, and sometimes as attention. It is easily included under both headings. Working memory is the ability to hold in mind bits of information presented simultaneously or nearly so, and to work with them so as to arrive at some integrated formulation. It is considered an aspect of attention because it requires attending to a number of things at once. An example of a task requiring working memory is solving an arithmetic word problem that is presented orally. One must listen to the entire statement, figure out the meaning of the question and the arithmetic operations to be employed, and simultaneously keep track of the numbers that are to be manipulated; and then one must do the required calculations without pencil and paper.

SOCIAL FACTORS

Strong social influences affect how a child approaches learning and how he comes to regard his successes and failures. Families are the major socializing agent in this regard, but schools also play a significant role. We will be considering environmental factors by looking at the influences upon learning that reside within the family and at school.

The Family

Some years ago, Lonnie Carton, a Boston psychologist, had a local radio program on families and child rearing. One day her subject was "The Four Ls of Parenting: Love, Limits, Listening, and Letting Go." There is both wit and wisdom in this alliterative mnemonic, and love and limits have special relevance to learning. Where learning is concerned, love has to do with what is given to the child in more or less direct fashion, and includes numerous forms of emotional support and intellectual stimulation. Limits have to do with what is expected of the child, and with the teaching of self-discipline; while this aspect of child rearing requires denial and sacrifice on all sides at one time or another, it too is a form of giving.

Love and Learning
Most parents know the importance of support, encouragement, and confidence building for their children. They can be counted on to express their pride and pleasure when a child has successfully accomplished a task or demonstrated in some other way that he is developing in hoped-for ways. However, many parents have difficulty finding a constructive response when a child is not performing as well as expected. Sometimes parents feel personally thwarted by a child's failure to do well, believ-

ing, and voicing the belief, that the child is lazy, doesn't care, or isn't trying. Everyone loses patience at times, but insults, name-calling, and inferences of not caring about school have a particularly negative effect. Some older children, who are truly confident of their abilities, can tolerate a certain amount of mean parental scolding, but for those who question their own competence, rightly or wrongly, the lack of parental understanding and help has serious consequences. Labels can become self-fulfilling prophecies, and children may give up on themselves, turning to nonachieving peers for comfort and company. On the other hand, parents are sometimes concerned that the child really is less competent than others the same age, or others in the family, and that concern gets in the way of offering positive, supportive assistance.

One of the most powerful ways for parents to build self-confidence in a child is to demonstrate their own confidence in her. For example, they can practice something with her until she masters it; they can remind her of what she used to not be able to do, but now can. If necessary, they can arrange for specialized instruction either in or outside of school. They can talk about their own school difficulties, communicating implicitly or explicitly that they got through a difficult time and know their child can do the same. This is often a shock as well as a relief to a child who sees parents as all-knowing and as always having been competent and successful.

Providing *intellectual stimulation* is another form of love that makes a significant contribution to children's learning. It is not just a matter of providing the early experience that is important for shaping neural development in the child's earliest years. When children have experience with problem solving as they handle their earliest toys, build with blocks, or play board games, they are discovering the intrinsic pleasure of intellectual mastery, as well as learning patience, persistence, and the frequent need to try again. Many activities, including listening to stories, looking at pictures, visiting animals at the zoo, and playing with refrigerator letters and numbers, build up stores of information and knowledge that make the schoolroom and school activities more familiar and welcoming than they would otherwise be.

After school entry, parents can demonstrate their support by encouraging burgeoning interests and introducing potential new ones that provide opportunities for the child to develop skills or special areas of knowledge. Even if a child's area of special interest and expertise is not entirely academic, it gives him standing and recognition in the eyes of his classmates, and in his own view of himself. Particularly for children who are not top students or who do not learn easily, the recognition and the positive facet of identity (that is, the sense of "one of the things about me is that I know all about _____") are particularly valuable.

Parents' failure to provide intellectually stimulating, enjoyable activities outside of school can put a child at a disadvantage relative to classmates and may contribute to a sense of inadequacy. Quick, high-achieving children may close the gap in good time; but for those who don't find reading or other aspects of learning easy, this is another obstacle to school success.

Limits and Learning

If there is going to be a parenting problem related to learning, it is more likely to be in setting limits than in providing material and emotional support. Many parents have a hard time denying their children a good time, enjoying the love and appreciation they see in their children's eyes when they gratify a desire, often against their better judgment. Sometimes they give up from simple exhaustion, worn out by the children's continued badgering. Where learning is concerned, limits usually have to do with making sure there is adequate time for doing homework. In many homes this means that parents must actively monitor, schedule, or restrict playtime, TV watching, and telephone use.

The interaction between parent and child around schoolwork can provoke a variety of difficulties. Many children having trouble with schoolwork try to keep that information from their parents as long as they can, particularly those in the upper grades. Parents are sometimes suspicious when they are told there is no homework or that it is already finished, but they may avoid looking into the matter, being no more eager than their child to confront an unpleasant reality. Often these parents avoid the issue, not out of lack of concern, but rather because of lack of confidence in their ability to provide suitable assistance, structure, or limits.

Other parents fail to set limits because they believe their children are too fragile or handicapped to be burdened by conventional school requirements. They try to make the children happy by relieving them of responsibilities, rather than strengthening their confidence and independence by showing them that they can do what is asked of them.

> *Will was a fourth grader of exceptional intelligence, with a relatively mild degree of dyslexia. He was reluctant to do his assigned reading from school and never read for pleasure. His parents were advised that some prompt, intensive tutoring could help Will overcome his reading difficulty fairly quickly, but Will didn't want to give up any of his after-school time, nor did he want to acknowledge that he had trouble reading. His parents were reluctant to press the issue because they didn't want to damage his self-esteem.*

This situation, in which parents accept a child's bravado and denial of difficulty as "self-esteem"—rather than recognizing it as a cover for poor self-esteem—is not uncommon. If the reading difficulty were faced directly and treated with appropriate remediation, genuine self-esteem would be raised, not only because of improved reading ability but also because of having faced up to a painful reality.

Parents of severely disabled children often learn this lesson more easily. In one family, a healthy, happy, successful fourth grader was suddenly diagnosed with a progressive crippling disease that soon confined him to a wheelchair. One day when he was complaining and feeling sorry for himself, his father said to him, "I know it's very hard, and it's certainly all right to complain, but don't make a career of it." This father was focused on developing emotional muscle in his son, so that the boy would be equipped to build himself a life based on competence and self-sufficiency to the greatest extent possible.

Family constellation is often a significant factor in how children feel about their ability to learn. Younger children with successful older siblings cannot help but compare themselves to the older ones, and for many of them, it does little or no good to remind them of the age difference. If the age gap is compounded by some degree of learning disability, it's easy for the younger child to develop a sense of not being like, or not being as good as, the rest of the family. Older siblings with reading difficulties are often dismayed to find they are surpassed by a younger child in the family, one who can read better in first grade than the older one can in third or fourth grade.

The School

In general, schools have not done well in helping children overcome reading difficulties. Although understanding of dyslexia has increased greatly in the past fifteen years or so, little of that has filtered through to elementary school teachers, to teacher training institutions, or to the publishers of elementary reading curricula (Blachman, 1996; Fletcher & Lyon, 1998; Moats, 1995b). Many special education training programs do not include any training in teaching reading disabled children (Cranston-Gringas & Mauser, 1992). I have been told by several special education administrators that none of the certified teachers they interview for their special classes has had specific coursework in teaching reading disabled children. This situation exists in spite of the fact that learning disabled children are the largest category of children in special education classes, and that among the learning disabled, the largest group by far are the reading disabled.

Regular education reading programs are designed for the majority of children, who will learn to read under almost any curriculum. In some instances these programs include some direct instruction in phonics, but in many others there has been little or no teaching of the code, and so children who cannot pick up the code quickly (that is, with little repetition or practice) or intuitively have been left to stumble along on their own. There is a strong tendency among teachers to view all early reading difficulties as "developmental," in the sense that they will be outgrown with further development. Indeed, almost all are *developmental* problems, in the sense that they are constitutionally part of the child rather than *acquired* as a consequence of disease or injury. However, as noted in Chapter 3, this does not mean they will be outgrown without intervention.

Among those who do not master the code and reach automaticity by fourth or fifth grade, some will be competent enough in other ways to mask their weaknesses and not be identified as having a reading problem. Those who are identified are shifted to the responsibility of some ancillary remedial program, which might be with a reading specialist and might be with a more general special education teacher who heads a resource room or learning center.

Toward the end of first grade, Steven was identified at school as having reading difficulties. In second and third grade he got about two hours of resource room help per week, spending the rest of his time in his regular classroom. The remedial program used by the resource room teacher suited him badly, and in fourth grade a new resource room teacher shifted him to a more effective program. While he made somewhat better progress there, his parents finally became alarmed and sought an evaluation outside of school. The evaluation showed him to be reading at first-grade level and to have a severe reading disability. A subsequent meeting at school revealed that much of the resource room time over the years had been used to help Steven do his regular classroom assignments, the argument being that it was important to keep up his self-esteem.

It is not uncommon for special educators to be caught in the dilemma of having to choose whether to devote their limited amount of tutorial time to filling in the gaps (in this case, helping Steven learn to read), or to helping the children do their classroom assignments. The children almost invariably want help with assignments so that they can feel successful in class. Classroom teachers know that children like Steven cannot do the work that is assigned to the class, but they haven't the time or perhaps lack the skill to prepare modified and useful assignments for them. In addition, teachers, like parents, are happy to see a child pleased at being able to turn in regular assigned work, even if they know that he is incapable of doing the work on his own.

While in the minority, some children are less concerned with the success of the moment, and are worried about their inadequate reading skills.

> *Paul was in the ninth grade, reading at about fifth-grade level. He was mildly to moderately dyslexic, but personal and family emotional problems had added to his distress and unhappiness, and although he had managed to remain in the public schools, with special education assistance, he could not tolerate the pressure and embarrassment he experienced once he entered high school. At that point he was referred to a private school for disturbed children with learning problems, and he made it clear to the staff there that he wanted to become better at reading, spelling, and writing. When he was asked by a staff member if he had received help with reading at public school, he explained, "I went to the resource room, but they did my work for me; they didn't teach me how to do it."*

Paul may have been exaggerating about getting no help at all with improving his skills, but he certainly was not getting enough appropriate help. As students get older, some of them are better able to assess and acknowledge their need for help.

They are more mature emotionally, and as they face the impending end of formal education, reality sets in. This provides some counterbalance to the inadequate assistance they may have received earlier.

PSYCHOLOGICAL FACTORS

For the most part, personality styles and emotional problems are not relevant factors in learning to read if one is not dyslexic. Difficulties in maintaining emotional stability or in getting along with others appear to affect reading acquisition only among children with constitutional deficiencies in the required skills. Then, in contrast to the emotionally stable dyslexics who will persevere or ask for help, those who are less sturdy psychologically will have difficulty staying with the task and will find many ways to avoid it. Because much of the treatment for dyslexia consists of repeated practice, the inability to persist is a major obstacle for these students when it comes to learning to read.

Two groups of students who have difficulty with persistence because of emotional problems are the severely emotionally disturbed, who are truly incapable of keeping their attention on their work, and the much larger group of children who lack motivation to achieve because of a variety of temperamental, family, and situational variables.

Chris had severe emotional problems that generally took the form of withdrawing into fantasy. He was a quiet, very intelligent boy, with severe dyslexia in addition to his emotional problems and chaotic family life. He entered a school for disturbed children at the age of 8 and remained there for eight years. He had individual tutoring in reading from the time he entered, but in his first few years there he could hardly keep his eyes on the page. He made very little progress in reading during those years, but he did develop a very close and trusting relationship with his tutor. In time, with the help of dedicated teachers and therapists he did learn to read well enough to tackle almost any text.

Motivation

The most common psychological factor that interferes with learning, including full mastery of reading if it has not been achieved in the early grades, is poor motivation. Up until the fourth or fifth grade, student work is closely directed in the classroom. The children are engaged largely in learning skills, and their work is laid out for them and monitored by the teacher. In addition, they are still at an age when teacher approval is of primary importance to them. Beyond that point they are expected to use their skills to generate sentences and paragraphs. This requires them to develop and put forth their own ideas, as well as to demonstrate how competent they are in the basic skills. They are also expected to take more responsibility for themselves—copy down assignments from the chalkboard, hang on to loose papers, keep their notebooks in order, bring in homework on time, and start long-term assignments before the last minute.

It is in the upper elementary grades that problems of motivation are likely to begin appearing among children who find it difficult to put themselves to work, to formulate ideas of their own in which they have confidence, or to take responsibility for keeping themselves and their possessions organized.

Frank was such a youngster. He had mild dyslexic difficulties that were first noted in third grade but viewed as too minor to warrant special attention. In fourth grade he received special attention in the form of warmth and understanding from his classroom teachers, but no help with skills; his handwriting and spelling at that time were very poor, and his reading was dysfluent. Affable in school, large for his age, and an excellent athlete, he got along well with everyone there. In fifth grade, things fell apart. The teachers were less interested in him, viewing him simply as a mediocre student who turned in poor work but behaved well and got along well with classmates. His parents saw him as considerably more able and were on his case at home, berating him for not trying harder and expressing their disappointment in him. They described him as irritable, unhappy, and failing to put any serious effort into his homework. An evaluation at this point revealed Frank's very good intelligence and mild dyslexia, along with his discouragement and pessimism about ever being able to achieve reasonable academic success. The parents were surprised and sympathetic when they understood his difficulties, and the school staff rallied around, giving him intensive help with the reading specialist as well as modified classroom assignments. A while later his father reported "a first"— Frank had come to him one evening, wanting his dad to listen to the beginning of a composition he was preparing for school.

For Frank, this episode marked a new attitude about school and its possibilities for him. Whether he could continue along these lines depended on many things: Would his parents continue to be supportive when the inevitable setbacks occur? Would the school staff remain attuned to his educational requirements, giving him necessary support but not making it too easy for him? Would Frank be encouraged enough by his current successes to develop a basically positive view of his competencies as a student? Finally, would his new perspective be enough to make him an active, organized, and conscientious student?

Frank's motivational difficulties stemmed from a combination of weak skills and the failure of parents and teachers to realize that he needed more understanding and assistance from them. He had already demonstrated that he was capable of working hard and taking responsibility in other aspects of his life. The outlook is less optimistic for students whose lack of motivation is not limited to school, but who show no interest in any artistic, intellectual, athletic, or social group activity. This condition is more likely to occur among adolescents than younger children, and it is an indication that depression, anxiety, or both are interfering with normal functioning.

> *Martin was in the ninth grade when his parents asked for a reevaluation. He'd been seen initially as a third grader, at which time he demonstrated very high intelligence along with some mild dyslexic characteristics. He received remedial assistance, and with continued support and high motivation to succeed on his part, his academic performance improved steadily until the middle of eighth grade. At that point things suddenly fell apart; his schoolwork took a downward plunge, he became increasingly withdrawn and uncommunicative with his parents, and he spent his time alone or with a small group of friends who were poor students. His parents reported that there had been a frightening event during the eighth-grade year, just before the change in Martin. A group of boys had severely beaten Martin's close friend while the two of them were out together in the neighborhood.*
>
> *When Martin entered high school six months later, he did very poorly in his classes. Moreover, he refused to participate in any extracurricular activities although he had always enjoyed sports and had other interests including chess. The reevaluation testing indicated that while he had the necessary skills for his schoolwork he was desperately anxious about his physical safety. He steadfastly denied any fears on this score or any other, and insisted that he could do perfectly well if his parents would only leave him alone. For the next half year he continued to fail at school, avoided academic support there, and refused psychotherapy. Then, finally, when he could no longer delude himself that he could manage*

on his own, he asked for help and began to work with a therapist.

With rare exceptions, all children want to do well at school. Most of the motivation problems around schoolwork result from children's discouragement about their ability to do well enough. Until fifth or sixth grade, parents and teachers are in a good position to take the necessary steps to restore confidence, largely through concrete academic assistance and moral support, and children tend to respond with renewed motivation to succeed. Later, as adolescents become acutely sensitive to their place in the social order and start to define their identities, they are heavily influenced by their peer group—either the one they wish to be part of, or the one they feel consigned to by default. More and more, their sense of who they are and wherein lies their worth come to depend on their view of where they fit in the social milieu. Under these circumstances parents have a very hard time providing help to children who have decided that doing homework isn't really important or that they aren't studious types.

Given the effects of biological, social, and psychological factors impinging on a dyslexic student, it is clear that a student's success will be heavily influenced by many circumstances in addition to dyslexia. Thus it is that in so many cases, a severely dyslexic child finds greater academic success and personal satisfaction than a child with a mild handicap who is encumbered with other circumstances that make his dyslexic burdens seem insurmountable. It is often difficult for parents of mildly dyslexic children to realize they must take a deeper, more comprehensive view of their child's personality and life circumstances if they are to offer the greatest possible assistance.

▶ 5

Impediments to Reading Comprehension

Reading comprehension—the ability to understand what has been decoded—is a competency that develops naturally in most readers. When children are first learning to read, they are less likely to have difficulties in comprehension, because the material they read is based on vocabulary and concepts that are thoroughly familiar, and content is presented in short, simple sentences. As a rule, only children who do not understand language in its spoken form, either because they are not native speakers or because they suffer from severe language disabilities, will demonstrate reading comprehension difficulties in the early grades.

However, there are many potential impediments to reading comprehension that begin to surface around third or fourth grade, and sometimes do not become evident until high school. Two of these are specifically related to learning disabilities. One results from dyslexia and is described first below. The second results from a combination of other learning disabilities and is more difficult to identify than dyslexia; it will be discussed later in this chapter. Other impediments to reading comprehension discussed in this chapter have to do with a variety of biological, social, and psychological factors.

READING COMPREHENSION DIFFICULTIES STEMMING FROM DYSLEXIA

Weak decoding skills are a common cause of poor reading comprehension. Of course, if a child cannot decode words and cannot recognize enough whole words to allow him to correctly identify strings of words on a page, we do not say this is a problem of reading comprehension. We say that he cannot read. However, many children have enough decoding skill and sight vocabulary to make their way through text, but are not skilled enough to get the gist of the material while they are engaged in decoding. In some cases, they misread so many words that they can't understand what is written. In other cases, their rate of decoding is so slow that by the time they come to the end of a sentence or paragraph, they cannot recall enough of what has come before.

These children, whose reading is either inaccurate or too slow, are often identified only in the later grades, if in fact they are identified at all. In the first few grades of school, when children read aloud in their classrooms, the teachers are aware of the slowness or the errors, but they do not consider these to be significant problems warranting assistance. There are many reasons why teachers may take this position, including: (1) the belief that the children will improve over time; (2) the belief that they are simply weaker students and that their reading is consistent with their general ability level; (3) the presence in class of children who have greater difficulty reading and who therefore receive any remedial help available.

The problems of many of these children come to light in middle school or high school, when the reading requirements are more demanding. They are expected to read far more material than in their younger days, and the material they read is more complex. There is more information packed into individual sentences and paragraphs, and students can no longer get by with gathering the general gist and making intelligent guesses. Some people complete their entire education without knowing what makes reading such an unpleasant chore for them.

Anita was one of those children whose reading disability, probably mild, was never recognized while she was in school. She requested an evaluation when she was in her mid-50s, in the midst of a very successful career, including a tenured college position and the publication of a highly praised book. She said that she had considered getting an evaluation for many years, but her embarrassment about her self-perceived inadequacies and her anxiety about having these measured had kept her away.

Anita said she read very slowly and often had to reread in order to get the full meaning. She reported that she had been slow to learn to read as a child, in contrast to her older sister who was an excellent reader. One teacher in particular in the early grades had been especially critical and unsympathetic, and Anita commented now, with some bitterness, that her parents had been on the teacher's side.

The evaluation showed her to have a superior vocabulary and good decoding skills with single words; however, her oral reading of text lacked fluency, with a number of small word substitutions and misread words. In Anita's case, the mild reading disability did not lead to academic failure; it did, however, become a major element in creating feelings of inferiority compared to other students, and a sense of not fitting into the family. Had the problem been identified early, it probably would have led to remedial intervention and subsequent improvement. It almost certainly would have affirmed to Anita her very high general abilities and spared her

many years of unhappiness generated by feeling glob-
ally inadequate rather than specifically handicapped
by a mild and narrow-gauged weakness.

Months after the evaluation was completed, Anita
called to say that she had been notably affected by what
she learned from it. Although her husband could not
understand what his talented wife had been so dis-
turbed about, nor what had happened to change her
perception of herself, understanding the obstacle that
had blocked her way made a great difference to her.

READING COMPREHENSION DIFFICULTIES RELATED TO ATTENTION

Most people have had the experience of reading along effort-
lessly and suddenly realizing that they have no recollection of
what they have read. In general, they are immediately aware
that their mind has drifted to other thoughts, while the decoding process has been proceeding with full automatization.
This is a normally occurring event and not considered a problem of reading comprehension, as no real effort has been put
forth to understand the text.

In considering attention problems that interfere with reading comprehension, it is in the context of a reader making an
active effort to attend. Many things can interfere with the
maintenance of attention, including the biologically based
deficits noted in Chapter 4. Children who have trouble attending to the presentation of information in other forms of
communication, such as lectures or films, are probably also
prone to attention problems during reading.

In addition to physiologically based poor self-regulation,
there are also failures of attention that stem from poor emotional control. Most of us have had the experience of trying to
concentrate on written material and finding that other
thoughts keep intruding in spite of our best efforts. Sometimes
we rally sufficient mental control and attend to the material,
and sometimes we put it aside for another time. Students have

the same kinds of experience, but they are under more pressure than most adults. They are working against a deadline much of the time, with assignments often due the following day. In addition, they often must read material not of their choice and of little or no intrinsic interest to them; the lack of engagement further strains attention.

Another variety of emotional interference with attention arises from the anxiety most typically associated with taking exams. That is, some people become so anxious about their ability to understand and remember what they are reading that they cannot devote enough steady, neutral attention to the task.

Less common is a more severe kind of emotional disruption in which the reader has far less ability to exert mental control over the thoughts and feelings that are evoked when reading. Sometimes the reader brings preoccupying concerns that he cannot shake as he picks up a book and tries to focus on it. Instead, his preoccupations interfere with attending to the book. In other instances, tangential ideas are triggered in the reader's mind by the content of the written material, so that he cannot stay engaged with the flow of ideas presented by the author.

READING COMPREHENSION DIFFICULTIES RELATED TO THE NATURE OF THE MATERIAL

Many problems of reading comprehension are directly related to specific aspects of the material being read, and the lack of fit between it and the reader. These problems usually stem from the fact that the reading material requires more knowledge, life experience, linguistic development, or literary sophistication than the reader brings to the task.

Knowledge

This includes vocabulary, factual information, and abstract concepts. In order to comprehend the general meaning of what they are reading, readers have to understand the meaning of the specific words in the text and must have some prior acquaintance with the concepts imbedded in the material.

Life Experience

This category is an extension of the previous one, but is less dependent on school-related learning and specific knowledge, and more a matter of personal experience. Prior experience with an array of people and places enhances your ability to connect what you are currently reading with other things you have read, seen, or heard about. Learning proceeds in large measure by accretion. We are collecting knowledge and experience in bits and pieces all the time, and much of it lies fallow until we get enough data, or just the right input. Added to what we already know, the new information provides a new, significantly greater degree of understanding. If, on the contrary, what you read about is totally unfamiliar to you, you will have a hard time assimilating the new information if there is no discernible connection between it and what you already know.

Linguistic Development

This category has to do with one's ability to handle longer and more complex phrases and sentences. Children's earliest verbal communication is generally organized in the sequence of subject-verb-object: "I want candy," "Jimmy hit me," and the like. Their earliest reading books follow this pattern. Language production and reading materials gradually develop into longer *strings* of words ("I want candy and ice cream." or "Jimmy hit me and I cried.") and into strings with progressively more complex sentence structure, including dependent clauses ("The man who was taking the clothes to the cleaners passed by a truck that had gotten stuck in the middle of the road.") and sequences of events that are stated in nonchronological order ("I couldn't get to the train on time because Joe had asked me to make three phone calls before I went anywhere."). As sentence structure becomes more complex, there is greater distance between the beginning and the end of a thought, with additional information in the middle that requires the reader's attention while he is still keeping track of the main idea. Here is an example from Henry James, by no means one of his longest or most complex sentences, but long and complex enough to illustrate how reading comprehension is taxed under these conditions:

> *It was the handsome girl alone, one of his own species and his own society, who had made him feel uncertain; of his certainties about a mere little American, a cheap exotic, imported almost wholesale, and whose habitat, with its conditions of climate, growth, and cultivation, its immense profusion, but its few varieties and thin development, he was perfectly satisfied* (Wings of the Dove, *p. 110).*

We have to hold our breath metaphorically until reaching the end of the sentence, to find out that he is satisfied about his certainties regarding the American, and if we have maintained even greater attention and memory, we will relate that fact to the first segment of the sentence, in which uncertainties about the handsome girl of his own species have been set up in contrast.

Literary Style and Sophistication

Adding to the comprehension burdens created by complex sentence structure are those that result from matters of literary style and range of content. The James quotation presents these difficulties along with those of linguistic complexity. To appreciate adequately what this sentence conveys requires some previous awareness about the attitudes of the English upper classes toward upstart Americans. Also, aside from the sophisticated vocabulary, sentence complexity, and social-historical context, the reader is required to manage this style of writing, in which main plot lines are interrupted by other material such as social commentary and character development.

While students are rarely asked to tackle reading matter as complex and demanding as the works of Henry James, they face comparable difficulties at their own level. Textbooks may present information that depends for understanding on prior knowledge that the student does not have. Literature may include paragraphs or even chapters describing the beauties of nature or relating historical background while the student is waiting for the narrative, wanting to know what happened to the characters he was reading about earlier. Students interested only in major plot outlines will fail to take in the other aspects of life that the author is conveying.

READING COMPREHENSION DIFFICULTIES STEMMING FROM OTHER LEARNING DISABILITIES

There are some individuals whose reading comprehension difficulties stem from some combination of learning disabilities, very often excluding dyslexia. That is, although their learning disabilities do not impair their decoding abilities, they do have a negative effect on their ability to comprehend fully or quickly what they read. In general, the contributing learning disabilities fall into the broad category of *language-processing problems*, which influence how well one can take in, absorb, and retain information presented via language. An often-ignored aspect of language processing is *visualizing*, the making of a mental picture to accompany the words.

Language processing is a large umbrella term, encompassing the many ways in which language is part of a chain of communication, with others and with oneself. Language is "processed" when you take it in (the input stage) and when you emit it (the output stage). The major forms of language input are listening and reading; correspondingly, the major forms of language output are speaking and writing. Between input and output, a great deal of language processing, including visualization, goes on in the mind as you gather the meaning, instantly or with effort, of what you have just taken in.

Much of the difficulty experienced by those with language-processing weakness has to do with the accuracy and speed at which information *comes to mind*. In language processing for reading comprehension, words seen on the page trigger associations with "language material" already stored in the mind; this language material includes word meanings, prior knowledge, and abstract concepts. In addition, verbal reasoning and organizing are activated, putting the associative bits of information into logical and grammatical order. For most people all of this occurs with a high degree of automaticity and little or no conscious effort, unless the material to be understood is highly unfamiliar or complex. People who are very good at crossword puzzles and other word games demonstrate highly effective language processing in which useful, relevant associations not only come to mind but *spring* to mind.

If you are a skilled reader with good comprehension, you can grasp what it's like to be weak in language processing if you know a foreign language well enough to get by, but lack true fluency. You read more slowly than in your native tongue, more words are unfamiliar, and it takes time to come up with their meaning. Idioms may take longer to figure out, and sometimes rereading of a sentence or paragraph is necessary to digest what you have been reading. In short, understanding does not come easily and automatically, and so you must proceed more slowly and with greater conscious effort. It has often been remarked that for dyslexics who have trouble mastering the code, and for those with reading comprehension difficulty related to language-processing weakness, learning to read and write in their native tongue is very much like learning a foreign language.

For those whose reading comprehension difficulties stem from weakness in visualizing, what fails to come to mind while reading are mental pictures, or what one sees with the mind's eye. Below are the opening paragraphs in a Wallace Stegner novel. As you read them, note that you are forming visual images, and consider whether you would be able to comprehend or be interested in what you are reading without those mental pictures.

> *Throughout the latter part of the morning buggies kept turning in from the highway and wheeling up the quarter-mile of elm-arched drive to the farm—surreys and democrat wagons, an occasional brougham, an even more occasional automobile whose brass caught the sunlight between the elms. By eleven o'clock there was a long line parked hub-to-hub against the tight windbreak of interlocked spruce at the north and west of the yard, and the house hummed with the subdued noise of many people.*
>
> *Sitting at the parlor window, old Mrs. Margaret Stuart had the whole yard, the drive, and the highway beyond under her eye. She could see the white tape of the state road looping over a low hill a mile to the west, the white gabled house and high-shouldered red barn of her neighbors the Paxleys, the cornfields standing dry and stripped in the thin October sun. Along the road clouds of dust crawled slowly, blown by no wind, almost obliterating the vehicles that raised them. Most of the dust clouds paused at the corner, hung briefly at the end of the elm tunnel, and resolved themselves into the dark moving miniatures of carriages or cars, to draw up at last in the growing line against the windbreak* (Remembering Laughter, pp. 1–2). Copyright © 1937 by Wallace Stegner. Copyright renewed © 1965 by Wallace Stegner. Reprinted by permission of Brandt & Brandt Literary Agents, Inc.

Not all written passages lean so heavily on visual imagery for understanding, but much of what we read does stimulate some degree of visualization. Lack of intuitive and automatic visualizing is a component of some learning disabilities, and it often underlies comprehension difficulties.

Barbara was a student who had weaknesses in language

processing. When her parents sought an evaluation of her academic difficulties, they were not aware of her difficulties with reading comprehension, although they knew she didn't enjoy reading.

Barbara was 14 years old and midway through the ninth grade when she was referred by a family friend, Kathy, who had known Barbara well over the years, and was a learning specialist by profession. Kathy had never worked professionally with Barbara, but she was familiar with the youngster's behavior patterns, study habits, and academic successes and weaknesses. Although the school had never recommended an evaluation of Barbara (and it was a school that referred many children for evaluation), Kathy encouraged the parents to take this step.

The parents described Barbara as an energetic, sociable, generally happy girl. She enjoyed sports and was active in school social service projects, helping out in centers for the elderly and for homeless children. She was a very diligent, conscientious student, but she was becoming increasingly discouraged by her lack of success relative to the time and effort she put in. Her friends tended to be among the highest academic achievers in the class, and it was a further source of dismay to her that they were doing better with less effort. She had begun to talk about being dumb, but at the same time she was determined to persevere and was hoping that an evaluation would somehow enable her to do better.

Barbara's parents described her school difficulties as being principally in writing; she had always had a hard time putting her ideas on paper. They said she read pretty well, but wasn't very interested in it. They added that she had no sense of direction, even having trouble finding her way on foot to familiar places.

Her parents wondered if her current, very demanding school was the best one for her, and if she had some particular kind of learning difficulty. Each parent had a brother with learning disabilities, and the parents themselves both reported having trouble putting ideas on paper. Her father said, "My personality type is like hers—I get determined, and just do it to get it done. I don't want her to suffer the frustration I suffered."

At testing, Barbara proved to be a very pretty, friendly, emotionally responsive girl. She was serious, conscientious, and fully invested in working at all tasks. Furthermore, she could work with steady, quiet persistence for extended periods of time. Along with these positive qualities, there were two other notable characteristics: she worked at a slow, and sometimes very slow, pace, and she made frequent comments expressing lack of confidence and indicating anxiety.

Test results revealed many anomalies, the most striking of which were severe discrepancies between scores on different types of intelligence tests, and on different types of achievement tests. Barbara had scored well above the 90th percentile on an untimed paper-and-pencil test of intelligence consisting of brief questions and answers, and dealing largely with previously learned information. By contrast, she scored 40 to 50 percentile ranks lower on an intelligence test requiring problem solving with unfamiliar material, and the formulation of verbal responses to complex, orally presented questions. This discrepancy might have been considered a fluke if there had not been a similar discrepancy in a different but related realm.

School records indicated that Barbara did very well, again at the superior level, on the machine-scored, standardized national tests of academic skills, which presented short items. These were answered in a multiple-choice format requiring no formulation of a response. The contrast in this instance was with her school grades and teacher comments: while math and science grades were B and better, her English, social studies, and foreign language grades were in the C to B− range.

Teacher comments included the following: "weak participation in class discussion," "too literal," "too short answers on tests," "too general without details to back up statements."

An example of Barbara's difficulties in language processing is her response when asked to tell what "brave" means:

Barbara: I know to *be* brave, if someone *is* brave, is that brave—because you can be brave—no, you always have to say someone *is* brave.

Examiner: (certain that Barbara knew what brave meant, and trying to help her out of the dead end her confusion had led her to) Can you give a synonym for brave?

Barbara: Courage kind of—brave is more like you have courage to—well, no, I guess it's basically the same thing as courage.

One of Barbara's difficulties in this instance has to do with a poor intuitive sense of grammar. Most ninth-grade students know (or sense) that a synonym for *brave* would be *courageous* rather than *courage*, even if they cannot always label or distinguish between nouns and adjectives. Another word that took her a very long time to define was *nuisance:* (long pause) "Something that is—(pause of more than 75 seconds)—annoying, I guess."

Not all of Barbara's responses were so labored. Most of her answers came more evenly, although her response pace was generally slow. Otherwise, if such glaring difficulties in formulating her thoughts were frequent, she would have been identified years earlier as having language-processing difficulties. Barbara's major difficulty with language processing was in formulating a verbal response (the output). Her ability to comprehend what she read (the input) was compromised by the fact that the process was so slow for her, but given enough time and patience, she was able to understand material at a high level. Because it took her so long, however, she found reading burdensome rather than pleasurable.

Visualizing ideas was difficult for Barbara. Her parents' report that she couldn't find her own way to school was the first indication in the evaluation that weak visualization ability might be part of her learning problem. During the testing, Barbara had a difficult time when she had to deal with complex arrays of visual material, such as pictures or geometric forms. To accomplish the task, she was required to imagine a rearranged or altered perspective of the material. She could eventually solve nearly all of the problems, but she was always very slow to do so, requiring additional time or extra practice before she came to the solution that most people reach easily.

It appears that many of those who, like Barbara, have trouble organizing the visual materials that they see in front of them are also prone to have trouble visualizing the ideas that are presented to them through reading. As they read, images do not spring to mind that would help them to assemble, integrate, and often enjoy (as in the Stegner selection) the material being taken in.

Barbara presents no signs of pure dyslexia; in fact, she excels at the mechanical aspects of reading, spelling, and handwriting. She also has excellent rote memory for factual information, a skill frequently lacking in those with pure dyslexia. Her difficulties in language processing have to do with organizing the elements of language into larger conceptual frameworks. She does not have trouble at the level of letters and words. She has trouble when she has to arrange the words into fluent language as she attempts to express her knowledge and ideas to others, and when she takes in the words of others (written or spoken) and searches to make meaning, in part through visualizing.

Barbara's difficulties with language processing were significant, but they could often be overcome with extra time or practice. Later, as she gained more practice in certain activities, such as organizing a written report, she was able to work more quickly using learned patterns and routines. Formulating ideas when under pressure or when dealing with relatively unfamiliar subject matter continued to come slowly. She was very much helped by supportive parents, her excellent skills in other areas, and her ability to persist through difficult tasks.

Lorna's reading comprehension difficulties were similar to Barbara's, but their consequences were more severe, and she found different ways of compensating for them.

> *Lorna was in her early 20s when her psychotherapist, Dr. Smith, referred her for evaluation. Lorna had started seeing Dr. Smith a few months preceding the referral. She had a history of school difficulties from the elementary grades through college, and in addition, Dr. Smith noted that Lorna seemed to find talking difficult in therapy. She had trouble speaking up on her own initiative, and when asked questions her responses were very brief. She had entered therapy because of longstanding depression and anxiety about needing to pass the physical therapy licensing exam, which she had already failed three times.*
>
> *When Lorna came for the interview preceding testing, she appeared worried and anxious, but also very relieved to be telling her story. The nature of the interview process—direct, specific questions about material with which she was very familiar—seemed to make the flow of information easier.*

(Note: The material that follows is transcribed from notes made during the interview. The information given is in Lorna's own words, and connections have been added to put it in sentence form.)

> *Ever since I can remember I've had a hard time taking tests, learning, studying, but I could always get by. Now I've taken the licensing exam three times and failed. I meant to look into what the problem is, in college, but I kept putting it off.*
>
> *I learned to read OK, but I hated to read. I still don't like to read much—five pages and I'm bored. When my*

parents would make it into a little lesson, "read this much and give us a little report," I could do that. I always bought Cliff Notes in high school. I avoided reading a whole book.

In high school my parents wanted me to see a psychologist; they were having a hard time with me. I thought they should see someone. I was getting Cs in everything. They said I'd be a waitress all my life. In college they were more supportive. Once I was in physical therapy school they were encouraging.

I went to public school. I was in private school for a semester. My parents thought it would get me away from my friends. They were worried about drinking. There was alcoholism in both of their families. I liked it at private school. It was fun, I had a boyfriend, people loved me there. I didn't do well, but it helped me learn to study. There were small classes, fifteen at most. If you had a struggle, you could ask the teacher. I didn't ask much; I didn't like asking for help.

In physical therapy training, I did better in practical classes, where there was hands-on or a lab. I'd sometimes get confused between left and right, give the wrong directions to patients and they would correct me. I don't learn from just reading, or else I won't recall it later. I have to do it or see it. Sometimes when I was reading a textbook I'd stand up and figure it out on myself.

I made the physical therapy decision by my sophomore year in high school. I'm athletic, did a lot of swimming and soccer especially. I was having knee pain, and ended up spending a lot of time in the physical therapy department, and I volunteered there.

I love my job, working with the patients. And I'm good at it. People were amazed when they heard I didn't pass the licensing exam. I'll have to leave there if I don't pass it in the next few months. You can work there without a license for only a certain period of time.

During the testing Lorna had difficulty taking in questions that were long or complex, as well as with formulating answers. An example of the difficulty in expressing what she knows came with her effort to define *plagiarize*:

> *To do something the same as something else . . . (pause)*
> *. . . to copy. (Long pause—she seems to be finished.)*
> *[How would you use the word?] If I were to write a paper*
> *and copy something from the encyclopedia directly . . .*
> *(pause) . . . someone else's work . . . (pause) . . . and*
> *claim it as my own.*

Lorna's difficulties in visualizing were first hinted at when she mentioned her occasional left/right confusion. It came across more dramatically when she explained that she often couldn't understand her physical therapy texts until she stood up to work out the information in relation to her own body. In other words, she couldn't form an adequate mental image from the words on the page, and work through the problem using that image. In order to comprehend, she needed to "express motorically" what she read.

Lorna's challenges bring up the concept of "multisensory" experience in learning. This concept is a hallmark of the most intensive instructional programs for the learning disabled and involves using a variety of modes for both the intake and output of ideas. Lorna's need to try things out on herself provides a fine graphic illustration of the concept. She *sees* the places involved on the body, and *moves* to work out the ideas, rather than using a mental image to which she then puts words. On a test, after working out her ideas concretely with vision, touch, and movement, she can then more easily transcribe the solution into the verbal mode and mark her test paper.

We all make use of multiple senses at various times. Sometimes it is to enhance an experience—for example, when beautifully presented food enhances the experience of a meal, when the texture of food adds something to the taste. At other times it is to strengthen a learning experience that is otherwise weak or uncertain; some students routinely copy over their notes in order to "inscribe" the material more firmly in memory. Among adolescents and adults, many who don't have a good ear for foreign languages often want to see words written down. By contrast, those who have a good ear and a poor sense of grammar prefer to learn their foreign language through immersion in it, hearing it spoken around them. This allows them to learn the grammar through the direct experience of hearing and repeating the words in a live context. The majority of people, those who do not have a particular problem in either domain, will learn through either approach, and probably learn most quickly and effectively if they have access to both.

Lorna's case also illustrates the importance of establishing some positive identity focus in adolescence. She was very fortunate in discovering the field of physical therapy during high school, in a setting where she was given medical treatment, appreciated for her talents, and offered the opportunity to help others. Her experience in physical therapy was a marked contrast to her general sense of her abilities as a student. She commented at one point following the evaluation that after learning she had a language-based learning disability, she daydreamed about calling friends from high school and college to tell them she wasn't dumb, that there was a reason for her having had trouble with school. In spite of her embarrassed, self-critical self-image as a student, she was able to persevere in her pursuit of physical therapy studies, work, and pass the elusive licensing exam because she felt sufficiently committed, confident, and supported by significant adults regarding her goal to become a physical therapist.

Lorna's case had a practical and happy resolution. In light of her language-processing problems, she was allowed extra time for her licensing exam, and given a private room in which she could get up, move around, and work things out on herself. Lorna is hardly alone in her difficulty in processing directions related to body movement, along with more general reading comprehension weakness. Ruth couldn't follow the instructions of her high school gym teacher when the class did group exercises; Ann was an avid ballet dancer whose advancement was hindered by her inability to absorb quickly enough the choreographic directions called out in practice sessions. Beyond the specific matter of body movement, many of those who have trouble following a string of directions are having some difficulty in absorbing the meaning of the words or in developing the collateral visual imagery that would reinforce understanding and memory.

MORE ABOUT LANGUAGE PROCESSING

Although discussion of language processing comes up only in this chapter on reading comprehension, it should be noted that decoding is also part of the language-processing chain, the first step in reading input. In skilled decoding one deals at an automatic level with linguistic symbols, pairing graphic symbol and auditory symbol so swiftly that no active thinking is required. Many dyslexics who have difficulty mastering the code at an automatic level have no problems with the rest of the language-processing operations. It is only in handling the linguistic symbols, as distinguished from the ideas expressed in language, that they demonstrate a weakness. Conversely, many of those with comprehension difficulties, like Lorna, had no difficulty learning to decode. Then again, there are those who have trouble with both decoding and comprehension. When we move beyond reading, and consider output through written or spoken expression, the number of possible weaknesses and areas of strength increases. In short, language processing is multifaceted and complex, and one cannot assume that because there are difficulties in a given aspect, there are therefore difficulties in certain other aspects, or in all aspects.

▶ 6

Case Studies

These case studies demonstrate the mix of particular personal, family, and situational variables that make each person studied unique. At the same time each represents a large group of children, adolescents, or adults who struggle with reading. Some have families who provide consistent, persistent support, and some do not. There are instances of simple good luck, and of very bad luck. There are those whose character traits contribute to a successful outcome, and others who must persevere in the face of their self-defeating styles and choices.

ROBERT—MILD DYSLEXIA WITH COMPLICATING FACTORS

Robert was 7 years old and just finishing first grade when his parents sought consultation. At a routine parent conference, Robert's teacher told them that he would always have trouble in school, although she couldn't specify why. They thought of him as being quite a bright boy and were distressed at receiving this early prediction of a poor future at school. In addition, they were concerned about his self-esteem, in view of such comments as "I'm really stupid," and "I'm the only one in the class who can't do this."

The younger of two sons, Robert was described by his parents as a sensitive boy, somewhat shy about moving into new social situations. They saw his temperament as being somewhat volatile, particularly in comparison with Paul, his seventh-grade brother, who was very composed and even-tempered. In addition, Paul was an excellent student with many friends. Robert "worshiped" Paul, who in turn gave him short shrift.

Robert was physically adept and liked being active. Physically, he was a risk taker, climbing the highest tree and riding his bike very fast, but his parents felt that he used generally good judgment and was not heedless. He was somewhat impulsive, but neither that nor his high activity level were problems at school, where he was regarded as well behaved. He participated in team sports, where he did well but was not a leader. Robert's few close friends tended to be among the brightest and quickest in class. He liked having his friends over, but was reluctant to initiate a phone call to them.

His parents reported that Robert had no significant difficulties with eating, sleeping, or hygiene. He ate well but disliked sitting through a meal. He slept well, though he didn't always get to sleep easily. The only notable exception to even development in early childhood was in learning to talk. At age 2 he spoke only a few words, and when full language came it seemed to come all at once.

When Robert's mother brought him for testing, he was a tall, slender, handsome boy, well spoken except for some trouble pronouncing /r/ sounds. In the waiting room with his mother he had first assumed a look of nonchalance and then was mildly resistant about entering the office. Once inside he was friendly and cooperative. He worked steadily on all tasks, with no sign of restlessness or distractibility, and he was highly invested in doing well. He continued to express through offhand comments that he was embarrassed about being tested, and often made spontaneous remarks that demonstrated his general cleverness and his concern that I recognize him as a smart person. He made frequent references to his brother—for example, "Do you do older kids?" (Yes.) "Oh, cool, I can tell my older brother he has to come here, and that will really annoy him."

Robert's overall score on intelligence testing was at the 96th percentile, but the subtest scores making up his cognitive profile ranged from average to superior levels. His memory for rote information such as math facts was weak, as were some of his visual-processing skills.

Robert scored at the bottom of the average range on tests of basic school skills (arithmetic, reading, and spelling), with all scores in the 30th to 35th percentile range. His reading was highly dependent on sight word recognition because his decoding skills were weak. Although he demonstrated knowledge of basic aspects of the code, he had difficulty with words that required analysis. He made such common errors as reading *little* for *letter* and *sleep* for *spell*.

Robert's struggle with the word *cliff* is a good illustration of his decoding weaknesses. He made three attempts, each time capturing correctly some part of the word:

1. cloth. Here he has the initial consonant blend (cl, two consonant sounds blended together) but the vowel sound is wrong, and so is the final 'f' sound.
2. koff. He now has the /f'/ sound at the end, but he's lost the /cl/ blend, and the vowel is still incorrect.
3. kiff. The /l/ is still missing but he has the vowel right and the final /f'/ too. At this point he gave up trying.

The guesses, demonstrating inconsistent knowledge of the various code elements, indicate that he has not yet mastered the symbol-sound correspondences but that he is on his way. They also tell us that he cannot yet hang onto all the elements in an unfamiliar word as he makes his way through it.

To summarize the test results as they relate to Robert's reading, the indications of dyslexia are:

1. Test score discrepancies. Intelligence scores above the 95th percentile, and academic skill scores at the 30th to 35th percentile.

2. Observed processing difficulties. Although Robert's reading score was average for a late first grader, his unsteady processing and lack of code mastery show that he is overly dependent on Stage I reading (global word recognition) and that his decoding ability is far weaker than that of the average child at the end of first grade.

The additional complicating factors are:

1. Somewhat overreactive temperament, which he keeps under control at school, though not at home.
2. Overconcern about self-image, which makes him anxious about acknowledging weaknesses. A major factor in this concern appears to be his sense of inferiority in relation to his brother.
3. Parental ambivalence about getting help.

Based on this evaluation I made three specific recommendations. The first was for specialized tutoring to hasten the process of reaching mastery and automatization in decoding. The second was to schedule a meeting at school to discuss the testing results and see if a modification in the school program was indicated. The third was to develop avenues for making Robert more psychologically independent of his brother, with areas of accomplishment in which he could take pride.

The parents did not schedule a meeting at school, and I next heard from them two years later as Robert was about to enter fourth grade. His parents requested another consultation to discuss his reading scores on the standardized tests he had taken at the end of third grade. He had scored at the superior level on the vocabulary subtest, and at the average level on the reading comprehension subtest. They were concerned about the discrepancy between the vocabulary and reading comprehension results, and the implications that might have for his ability to learn.

I asked what had been going on with his reading since I'd seen him two years earlier. Robert's parents reported that he had worked with Betty, a specially trained reading tutor, early in second grade. Although he always complained about going, he seemed to enjoy the sessions, coming out happy after each lesson. When his school began to provide him with extra help later in the second grade, his parents dropped the tutoring. At the end of second grade he was declared to be a good reader and was not recommended for further help in third grade.

And so Robert had proceeded through his third-grade year with no supplementary reading help. He avoided reading, complained about it, and was very resistant to the idea of getting any help. When his parents told him that they were coming to see me and perhaps have him retested, he was adamant about not doing that, insisting that there was nothing wrong with him and that he didn't have a problem.

From the parents' report, the standardized test scores, and the earlier testing, I guessed that Robert had now pretty well mastered the code, but was having trouble with accuracy when he tried to read at a normal pace. That would explain his excellent score on the vocabulary subtest, which requires reading very few words in order to respond. Reading comprehension tests involve reading more extended text, so unless he slowed down to analyze unfamiliar words, he would be likely to misread. His mother said that when he read aloud at home he did make frequent errors—for example, he read *population* as *popularity*.

From the parents' report, I concluded that Robert did not need a full psychological and educational evaluation, but rather a careful assessment of his reading abilities. I assumed that he would need help first in slowing down in order to acquire accuracy; once his reading was accurate he could work for greater fluency. I recommended to the parents that they return to Betty for an updated reading assessment, or if they thought she was not a good match for Robert, we would locate another tutor. I did not suggest looking to the school for remedial help because there were no remedial services available for students whose test scores were at grade level. Although I am convinced that a boy with superior intelligence who hates reading and shows specific weaknesses is in need of special assistance, I do not believe in fighting with schools over their allocation of limited resources when I know the parents can afford outside help. In Robert's case, outside help is probably preferable anyway, because he cares so much about maintaining a good front at school.

Robert's parents repeatedly expressed concern about his self-esteem, stating that he took it very hard when he didn't perform as well as he thought he should. They tended to lean heavily on reassuring him that he was fine and soft-pedaling or denying any indication of weakness. In the most recent consultation meeting we discussed at length the probable causes of his reading weakness and his hatred of reading. I stressed the importance of attending to this mild problem early, as it is fairly easily remedied and early intervention can make a great difference as to whether a student will discover the pleasures of reading or continue to shun it whenever possible. Until reading becomes truly automatic as discussed in Chapter 2, it is work and not pleasure. Some children who are slow to achieve automatization will plug away at it until they do, but those who have difficulties such as inattention, restlessness, and anxiety will not persist if they can find a way out. Tony, an eighth-grade boy described in Chapter 3, whose reading difficulty went untreated and largely unrecognized, is a typical example of this group.

I did not hear from Robert's parents after this consultation. During our meeting they seemed persuaded that they should do something quickly and said they'd be happy to return to Betty rather than seeking out another tutor. A month later Betty had not heard from them. Not knowing the end of the story, we are free to speculate about possible outcomes. Perhaps they did eventually contact Betty or someone else, or they may have continued with the status quo, worried about Robert but unable to take action.

Robert is at risk, but it is important to recognize that he is not necessarily doomed to reading failure and a weak academic career. A classroom teacher may notice the weakness and do something herself to improve his skills, or perhaps speak to his parents about getting help. Robert may discover on his own, by falling in love with some special book, that reading offers him something enjoyable and is worth the additional effort it will cost him for a while. Although the odds are not in his favor, there have been people who had early reading difficulties and improved without remedial assistance.

SALLY—MILD DYSLEXIA WITH AMELIORATING FACTORS

Sally was in the second half of second grade when her parents took their concerns about her learning to their pediatrician, who in turn referred her to me for evaluation. The parents described her as a hard worker who struggled to accomplish grade-level work, especially in reading. She made many errors in reading as well as writing. Sometimes she wrote her name entirely backwards. Her parents expressed their goal for the evaluation as "we need to help her learn more easily."

Sally, $7\frac{1}{2}$ years old, was the second of four children in a family of high-achieving, professional parents. Her younger brother and sister were toddler-age twins. She had an older brother who was quick and agile, while Sally was affectionately described as a little klutzy, both in gross motor skills and in fine motor coordination. Her overall pace was slow, not only in schoolwork, but in other things too; she was a slowpoke in a household of fast movers. She participated in a number of after-school activities, including soccer, violin lessons, and drama, all of which she enjoyed although she wasn't particularly talented in any of them. She had a comfortable social life, with two or three good friends she played with most often.

Her parents said that Sally's development had been normal, with the exception of a bout of meningitis when she was two weeks old. Prenatal development and delivery, eating, sleeping, and hygiene were unexceptional. She was a precocious talker, talking in full sentences before her first birthday. They described her as emotionally sophisticated, intuitive, compassionate, and able to verbalize her feelings, although at times they thought she went too far when she became upset over little or nothing. They saw her as confident about speaking her mind and willing to try new things. She seemed unconcerned about her labored reading. She was remarkably persistent at it and proud of her effort. Her violin practicing followed a similar pattern; she was clumsy at it but persevering, and derived satisfaction from it for quite a while.

Sally was an attractive, well-formed child, with long, dark hair pulled back from her broad forehead. When she first came to my office for testing she was quite shy, but she became more relaxed over time. She was relatively quiet and serious throughout the three testing sessions, working hard and thinking hard. She worked very slowly, especially as she began each new task. Once she became more familiar with the task she often picked up speed, but her overall pace remained slower than average.

Sally scored above the 99th percentile on the verbal portion of the intelligence test, with abilities in reasoning and in understanding abstract concepts far beyond her years, and a very strong vocabulary and general knowledge base. Although not as striking as her verbal abilities, her scores on the nonverbal portion of the test were well above average. By contrast, her academic achievement scores were in the average range, with the reading score below the mean at the 32nd percentile.

Sally's reading score, while lower than expected, was still within the average range for her age group, which probably explains why she had not come to the attention of her classroom teacher. But she fell well below the average range in respect to mastery of the phonics code. The percentile score on the reading test is helpful in providing a "ballpark" estimate of where her reading ability lies relative to that of her classmates and her age group. It does not give information about how she manages to read or which skills are in place and which are not. That information comes from observing her at work, noting what she reads easily and accurately, what she reads incorrectly at first and then corrects, and what she does not seem to understand at all.

Most of Sally's errors involved poor visual processing of words that were not in her *sight vocabulary*. (Sight vocabulary consists of the words that children recognize as whole words, with no conscious effort of decoding.) Sally had a good sight vocabulary, which helped her along considerably. Her reading demonstrated the following difficulties:

She could not reliably do an accurate visual analysis, even working at her slow pace. On a list of first-grade words, she misread *away* as *anyway*, *seen* as *send*, and *cry* as *carry*. When asked to read each of these words again, she read them correctly. In general, she had some difficulty tracking through an unfamiliar word—thus, for *felt* she tried *flat* and then *fleet*.

She misread digraphs frequently, reading *chat* as *cat*, *thin* as *tin*, *shay* as *say*. Sally sometimes corrected herself after her first utterance, but she often failed to recognize the error.

Vowels were weak. Sally often confused short 'a' and short 'e,' and frequently failed to apply the "silent E" rule (which produces a long vowel sound: *hat* becomes *hate*, *sit* becomes *site*, *not* becomes *note*, and so on).

Test results confirmed her parents' belief that she was an intelligent girl with some specific difficulties that slowed her down, and they were eager to get assistance for her. A meeting at school made it evident that she would not meet the criteria for inclusion in the remedial program, although the teacher was sympathetic and offered to do whatever she could to help. The parents decided to arrange outside tutoring for Sally. A follow-up call to Sally's tutor a few years later revealed that Sally had overcome her reading difficulties within a year, after which she read fluently.

While Sally mastered the phonics code elements and achieved automatized, fluent reading in good time, she did continue to have difficulty with spelling. Spelling difficulties almost always accompany reading difficulties, and often they remain after reading fluency has been fully accomplished. In most cases, misspelled words are spelled phonetically, so that they can be deciphered by a reader, even if they are not spelled correctly according to convention—for example, 'ov,' 'pleez,' and 'Wensday.' These kinds of spelling errors indicate that the problem is one of visual memory rather than one of difficulty in sounding out a word or writing down the sound elements in the correct order. To understand what appears to be the major reason for continuing spelling errors once reading fluency and accuracy are accomplished, it is important to distinguish between two aspects of memory, *recognition* and *recall*. In reading, where the word appears in print, immediate visual *recognition* is required for fluency and accuracy. Spelling, on the other hand, requires that one call up, or *recall*, a visual image of the word, which is a more demanding memory task.

Robert and Sally both have mild cases of dyslexia, but Sally's skill development was weaker than Robert's although she was three-quarters of a year ahead of him in school at the time of testing. Although he had a lighter case of dyslexia than she did, and both received some assistance, she gained mastery and enjoyment of reading, and he did not. In addition to dyslexia, Robert was carrying a more emotionally reactive temperament, anxiety about appearing incompetent, and his parents' wish to spare him. Sally brought to the task a high level of motivation, a "plugger" temperament, and an absence of embarrassment at needing assistance. Her parents were eager to help her learn more easily and did not attach stigma to the idea of getting help.

These two children illustrate that factors other than the severity of the dyslexia play a major role in outcome. But they are illustrative also of patterns of differences between the sexes. Among the children whose learning difficulties I have evaluated over the years, it has been my observation that girls more often than boys are pluggers and enjoy rather than resent getting help, while boys more often than girls show a restless temperament and are more concerned with how they measure up.

BILL—AN ADULT WITH MODERATE DYSLEXIA

Bill, a golf pro and generally talented athlete, was 29 when he requested an evaluation. He had been referred by one of his clients, to whom he'd confided his long-standing unhappiness over his problems with reading, spelling, and expressing himself in conversation. Bill was single, and he split his year between Arizona and New England, working in the Southwest during the winter months and coming east when the weather turned warm enough for golf. He worked at golf clubs in both locations, giving lessons and longing to become a tournament-playing professional.

Bill grew up in a small southern town, the youngest of four children. His mother ran a small shop, and his father was plant manager for a large manufacturing company. Bill described himself as the only unsuccessful member of his family. Of his three siblings, two had been successful in school, and the third had dropped out of college but then found renewed interest and motivation to return and finish.

Bill's school difficulties began in the primary grades. "The school wanted to hold me back, but my father said no. We tried tutors but it didn't click." He struggled along, getting through high school with his mother's help. He played football at college, and quit school after two years following a football injury. "I wasn't getting anything out of it. I was there for the wrong reasons." In recent years he had tried to get help with reading, probably motivated by a requirement to take a written exam connected with his work. He ordered a phonics program he saw advertised on TV, he tried a night school class, and then individual tutoring, but nothing worked for him.

Bill described himself as lacking confidence, which he attributed entirely to his reading problem. He said he would be doing ten times better if his self-consciousness about his speaking, reading, and writing were not holding him back. He was critical of his coworkers because they were not moving ahead in the profession even though they didn't have his learning problems. (This attitude about reading being the source of any and all of his difficulties signaled a lack of self-awareness similar to that of people who believe that they would be completely happy and successful if only they were rich, beautiful, thin, brilliant, and so on.)

Bill's test results showed that he had average overall intelligence, with verbal intelligence in the low average range. Bill expressed himself well in ordinary conversation, talking about familiar topics. When he had to formulate a complex idea or deal with an unfamiliar or uncomfortable topic, his language became halting and fragmented, and he had trouble finding the right word. For example, when asked who was Martin Luther King, Jr.: "I wanna say black socialist but—he was trying to get the whites and blacks to come as one—would that be activist?"

Achievement scores showed reading of single words and arithmetic computation at about seventh-grade level and spelling at fourth. Reading displayed visual discrimination difficulties (*from* for *form*) as well as some difficulty in sounding out unfamiliar words. His spelling was largely phonetic (*musiom* for *museum*, *preshous* for *precious*), but occasionally sounds or syllables were distorted or lost (*sujection* for *suggestion*, *exetive* or *executive*). Thus in both reading and spelling he had problems of phonological and of visual processing. Bill complained of not being able to read quickly enough to get the captions and inserts on TV sports shows.

The reading test on which he scored at seventh-grade level required only the decoding of isolated words. He found reading text much more difficult. When Bill tried to read a paragraph on the sports page of the newspaper, he could not understand the content for many reasons. He stumbled over long or unfamiliar words such as *interminable* and *mythical*. Once he had decoded them, he was uncertain about their meaning. He could not read or understand the designation 1995–96. He tended to omit small words and suffixes, especially the final 's.' Also, the sentences were long and complex in structure and that, together with his slow reading, would make comprehension difficult even if he had been able to read accurately.

The testing showed that Bill knew the elements of the phonics code but that he was far from achieving the level of automaticity. For him, reading consisted of plodding through material. Bill had to devote so much energy and attention to decoding that he had trouble understanding what he had read. His lack of vocabulary, information, and experience with complex concepts also limited his comprehension. He read the newspaper only occasionally, and commented, "Sometimes I look at it and it's just a bunch of letters." When he read a newspaper paragraph with me he was totally discouraged by his failure to comprehend what he had read. Rereading it two or three times would have helped him, as it helps people who are learning a foreign language, but he was too debilitated by his failures to persevere over the long haul.

Bill's dyslexia involved both visual and phonological processing deficits. In addition, lack of exposure to more sophisticated ideas makes reading even more difficult, because it renders context a burden rather than an aid. Some people with dyslexia manage to maintain their intellectual development with little or no reading; they learn through television, movies, magazines with short articles and many pictures, and discussions with family, friends, and coworkers. Bill's social contacts were minimal, and he had few interests outside of his passionate wish to move up in the world of professional golf.

Although I learned a great deal about dyslexia from Bill, I am afraid the evaluation was not very useful to him. He was glad to know that his problem was of a recognizable and specific nature and not a matter of poor intelligence. However, he was disappointed to learn that he would need to work with someone over a period of time to gain the necessary practice in reading, and to develop his writing skills more fully. He was at some disadvantage in living in two different communities each year, but I was able to reach good professional tutors by phone in both locations and to give Bill specific names and phone numbers. Bill did not pursue these leads. His case is a

very sad example of the difficulty dyslexic adults have in working to improve their language abilities once they leave school.
Those who do succeed must be singularly motivated, and connected to tutors or other structured remedial programs and resources.

Bill's story also exemplifies those cases in which effective
reading requires more than basic decoding skills and reasonable intelligence, where achieving fully automatized (Stage
III) reading is dependent on social support and available remediation, and where personality factors can determine
whether one will persevere or not. This is the case with many
adults whose dyslexia was untreated or undertreated when
they were children. By contrast, children who are given remediation early enough to allow them to match their reading
skills with their conceptual ability will not turn away from
reading, so long as the material available to them is sufficiently interesting and matches their ability levels. For a while,
their continuing to read is dependent on the expectations and
support of their parents and teachers, but for the most part
they seem able to use reading as a manageable tool throughout their lives. As adults they may not love to read, but they
are able to read what is important to them. Even children with
severe dyslexia who do not receive help until adolescence can
develop sufficiently automatic reading to make it useful. I am
acquainted with two boys who were total nonreaders when
they began tutoring at age 12. One was James, mentioned in
Chapter 2, who could not identify the sound of 'ch.' In each case
it took about six years to become sufficiently fluent, but because they were still in school, they had the social and institutional supports necessary to keep them at the task. Bill,
unfortunately, did not.

EILEEN—AN ADOLESCENT WITH RECENTLY DIAGNOSED DYSLEXIA

(Note: Eileen's case was presented in somewhat different form
in an earlier work [Sanders, 1979].)

I met Eileen in the fall of her tenth-grade year. She was an attractive, high-spirited, outspoken, friendly teenager. She had a close group of friends and held down a part-time job in a local store. She enjoyed athletics, especially swimming, and hoped someday to become a marine biologist. She lived with her parents and older brother in a small, comfortable suburban community. Her mother had worked as a secretary at one time but now did mainly community service work, and her father was an engineer.

Eileen had appeared to be doing well in school, but in the eighth grade she revealed to her mother that she had great trouble reading. She never read complete assignments and had never read a whole, full-length book. She had begun to worry about how she would manage in high school and college. She knew marine biologists needed a college degree and was afraid that although she had gotten by so far through careful listening in class and a minimal amount of reading at home, this would not be enough to carry her in high school and college.

Up to that point, her parents had noticed that she had difficulty on the rare occasions when she read something aloud, and they knew that her spelling was poor. They had raised questions at school from time to time over the years about these weaknesses, but were always reassured by teachers that Eileen was doing well. After Eileen came to them, they requested an evaluation at school. That evaluation took place in the spring of ninth grade, but although a useful reading assessment was done, the school staff was unable to develop a remedial program for her. Eileen's mother explained in her introductory letter to me that "since the resource room specialists' experience has been with children whose problems were discovered when they were in the primary grades, they are hesitant to work with Eileen for fear they may do more harm than good." The parents asked me to evaluate Eileen's reading and suggest a remedial program for her.

The reading specialist at school had uncovered Eileen's basic difficulty: a motivated, sprightly ninth grader with above-average intelligence, Eileen was unable to recognize words automatically beyond third-grade level. She could read almost every word she encountered correctly, but she always required time to analyze them. She had mastered the code, but was exceptionally deficient in automaticity. When I saw Eileen her reading rate was 30–40 words per minute when she read popular, general material such as *Newsweek*. It was slower when she read from her biology textbook. This is excruciatingly slow reading. There are 29 words in the first three lines of this page. Normal reading speed is upwards of 250 words per minute.

Eileen had the capacity for good reading comprehension if her decoding skills became more automatized. Because she took so much time to decode each word, she found it difficult to remember what she'd read at the beginning of a sentence by the time she got to the end. In order to read and understand text at her pace, she had to go through each sentence slowly once, in order to sound out all the words, and then immediately reread the sentence one or more times with greater speed in order to comprehend the meaning. Only the most highly motivated and patient student will do this, unless perhaps a parent or teacher is sitting at her side providing encouragement and praise.

Eileen had made a practice of reading only to herself and by herself, because she was too ashamed to reveal her poor ability. Her habit was to read material once at a normal pace, skipping over any words that at first glance appeared unfamiliar or complex. With simple or somewhat familiar material, she could get by with intelligent guessing, but as she herself realized by eighth grade, this sort of skimming would not suffice for more advanced and difficult material.

Eileen's difficulties with language fell in a very narrow range involving visual recognition of the printed word. She spoke freely, had an extensive vocabulary, and also wrote easily in the sense of being able to speak her mind on paper with feeling and good organization. She needed practice in reading, of two types: (1) free reading of text, and (2) organized instruction that would familiarize her with recurrent elements of the language and thus help her recognize words more quickly. Some of that instruction would involve rote drill and some of it would involve a more interesting analytic process in which she would become more knowledgeable about language structure, including root words, prefixes and suffixes, and spelling patterns. This would enable her to more easily recognize complex words.

I recommended a minimum of three hours of reading practice a week and some reading every day. To help her get through her school texts until she could read more quickly on her own, I referred her to Reading for the Blind, which also makes available books on tape for those with dyslexia. Her parents asked the school to provide Eileen with a set of textbooks that she could mark up. That allowed her to highlight information and add her own signs while listening to the tapes, so as to reinforce important points and find them again when reviewing for tests.

Eileen was a proud, strong-minded girl, and like many high school students perceived that there was a stigma attached to getting help in the resource room. She stuck it out for a while doing some of the drill work and also using the time there to work on her homework assignments. But in a follow-up meeting in December of her junior year she told me, "I can't stand the resource room. I know the staff means well but it makes me feel awful." She stopped going, and received no more instruction.

In the meantime, however, she had begun to read on her own, starting in her sophomore year when her friends were reading and talking about a best-selling novel. One of her friends offered to read it to her, and Eileen retorted that she could read it herself. That night she stayed up until 3 A.M. reading. There's no telling how much of the book she actually read, but it was apparently enough to break the ice because after that she continued to read on her own. There was the occasional popular best-seller, the newspaper, and certain assignments that went more easily, such as Hemingway short stories that are high on drama, dialogue, and familiar vocabulary, and low on dense, descriptive passages.

Eileen continued this way through her senior year of high school, doing some reading and increasing her fluency up to perhaps 70 words per minute. This helped but did not come close to making her a fluent reader. She kept her part-time job throughout, and was coeditor of her class yearbook. She was accepted at several small colleges whose admissions officers were aware of her reading disability. My last contact with the family was a letter from her mother at the end of the first college year. She wrote that Eileen had enjoyed school and was looking forward to her sophomore year. She had received some assistance in reading her biology text during the first semester, but did not request a reader during the second semester, which resulted in somewhat lower grades. She was holding a C– average. Her mother wrote, "She admitted it was a bit difficult getting through the Sociology and Psychology texts. I'm hoping that next year she will look for assistance when she needs it."

Once her dyslexia was uncovered, Eileen's parents were active and persistent in seeking out assessment and remediation of her reading difficulty. At the same time, they recognized her strong will and insistence on making her own decisions. This can be seen in her mother's response when she was asked by a high school counselor, "What does Eileen like best about herself?" "Her ability to be herself and express herself." Her parents respected and perhaps admired this side of Eileen, and while they did not let her make her own decisions in all situations, they did try to let her make as many choices as possible and live with the consequences. Although they could encourage her to continue remedial work in high school and get reading assistance in college, at this stage of her life there was probably nothing to be gained by their insisting.

Eileen's dyslexia was less severe than Bill's, the nature of her difficulties were brought to light at an earlier age, she was in general a more confident person, and she received more effective assistance from both home and school. Nevertheless, she was significantly handicapped because her reading difficulty was not identified earlier. If her lack of automaticity had been noted in the primary grades she could have been scheduled for regular oral reading practice in the course of the school day or even after school. Elementary school students generally enjoy the extra attention and help, and, even had she balked, her parents probably would have made the decision for her. By fifth or sixth grade the peer group begins to play a prominent role in a child's perception of what is OK and what is not, and from then on it becomes increasingly difficult to force a remedial program on an unwilling student. In adulthood, people like Bill may decide for themselves that they need help. However, it is very difficult for adults to stay with a remedial program that will take a long time, does not fit easily into daily work schedules, and does not offer easy access to teachers or family members for frequent practice in reading aloud.

Here again we can see how the process of learning to read is analogous to learning to play a musical instrument. Children who want to learn to play an instrument often do not enjoy practicing. When they are young, their parents decide to make the lessons available, and for a while they monitor the practicing. After a time, if the child consistently avoids practicing or complains about it, parents may allow the child to quit or they may decide themselves that the investment in lessons is not worthwhile. Children who stop studying music often grow up to be adults who regret that they didn't stick with it as children. They feel it is too late for them to pick it up again. Similarly, children and adolescents who hide their reading weaknesses or balk at remedial instruction in their youth may eventually perceive the need for better reading skill when it is far more difficult to achieve. Unlike musical accomplishment, however, reading competence is an essential rather than an optional skill in our society, and to be without it has far more severe consequences.

Learning to read also differs from learning to play an instrument in that reading skill can be acquired far more quickly and with less intense effort. Technical mastery of reading is generally achieved by age 7 or 8, and those with difficulty require a few years more. Musicians must continue to improve and maintain technical competence with hours of daily practice throughout their careers. When one considers that children have years in school to become competent readers, and that for some that opportunity is missed through lack of awareness and preparation within the educational system, it seems a huge and unnecessary loss. Bill and Eileen are examples of this kind of loss, young adults who as children had mild to moderate difficulties that were not recognized or understood and attended to.

NICHOLAS—MODERATE DYSLEXIA WITH EARLY INDICATORS

I met Nicholas when he was $7\frac{1}{2}$ years old and nearing the end of first grade. His parents were very concerned about plans for the coming school year. He had not done well in first grade, he was often unhappy about school, and the school was recommending that he repeat first grade. The parents explained that they were perplexed as well as worried. Although their son had been evaluated twice in the previous two years, they were still in the dark as to the cause of his poor school performance. They described him as a sweet, accommodating child whom they believed to be quite intelligent.

Nicholas was the younger of two children. His parents were well educated and his sister was a successful student. All reports from teachers and evaluators noted what a personable and friendly boy he was, with no behavior or attention difficulties. He was motivated to do well, worried about tasks that he found difficult, and was very happy and proud of his successes.

Nicholas was born eight weeks premature, weighing four pounds, and he spent more than three weeks in neonatal intensive care before going home. He was slow to eat and gain weight, but with the exception of asthma he had no chronic medical problems and was generally in good health at the time of this evaluation. He was the smallest child in his first-grade class, and in the lowest 5 percent on height and weight charts for his age group.

At age $5\frac{1}{2}$, in the spring preceding kindergarten entry, Nicholas was evaluated by a group specializing in preschoolers. He had been referred there by his preschool teacher because of difficulties in language development. She noted that his articulation of sounds was poor enough that he could not always be understood, and he had trouble with complex communication. For example, he could not follow multiple instructions (receptive language) and had difficulty expressing complex ideas (expressive language). In an eighteen-page report, the evaluation team confirmed with standardized assessment measures that Nicholas was indeed weak in these areas. They also assessed his foundations for reading development and reported that he did not recognize rhyming sounds or identify words beginning with the same letter sound. They found his vocabulary to be weak and noted his difficulty in finding words to express his ideas. They characterized him as having language-based learning disabilities. They did not mention dyslexia, which is not surprising as he had not yet entered kindergarten. Unfortunately, neither his parents nor his kindergarten or first-grade teachers could grasp the implications of the report findings well enough to make the connection between them and his poor school achievement.

Based on that evaluation, Nicholas received speech therapy for articulation problems, but his other language problems were not given any particular attention. Nicholas entered kindergarten, his weaknesses persisted, and toward the end of the school year he was evaluated at school. This evaluation was more sketchy, did not investigate language abilities, and did not make further recommendations. Nicholas then entered first grade, and as the school year ended with the recommendation to repeat first grade, the parents went looking for answers a third time.

When I met with Nicholas I found him to be a handsome and engaging little boy. He related well but was worried about not doing well. His speech was fully intelligible, although he did not enunciate all sounds clearly. Most prominent was his difficulty with the 'th' sound, resulting in 'mouf' for *mouth*, and 'frow' for *throw*. His spoken language showed weak vocabulary, and problems in constructing phrases and sentences to express his ideas. Here are some examples of language deficiencies:

> He did not know the word *triangle* when naming a number of shapes.
>
> He did not know the meaning of the word *season* but understood the concept. When told that winter was one of them, he named the other three.
>
> (Explaining the sequence of pictures he had just arranged) "The guy has a match, he puts it on fire, the fire people come, and they get the fire away."
>
> (For a dresser knob or handle) "One of the things you push open and close."
>
> (Umbrella) "Something that it stops rain from coming on you."

In reading, Nicholas had a small sight word vocabulary, and he knew the process of sounding out words letter by letter. However, he did not know the short vowel sounds, which left him helpless to sound out an unfamiliar word. He did know the consonant sounds, but had not mastered pronouncing words that began with two consonants, such as *block* which he read as *bell*. He could blend two consonants sometimes, as with the word *plot*, which he read first as *plat* and then as *plate*. Overall, his reading skills were at early first-grade level. When I told the parents he had dyslexia, they expressed relief at having a name for his problems.

Nicholas had broad weakness in language, both spoken and written. When he himself was speaking he had trouble calling to mind the correct names for things, which added to his difficulty in putting together sentences according to conventional language usage. When he was the listener he had difficulty taking in and retaining lengthy spoken communications, such as a set of directions. Once he had learned to read he would become less dependent on remembering what was said. In addition, through reading and rereading he would gain more practice with vocabulary and usage, and in this way be able to increase his language fluency.

In the meantime, Nicholas was not learning to read at a normal pace. As Nicholas was the smallest child in his class, we can perhaps understand the school's recommendation that he repeat first grade. But the school, not recognizing Nicholas's language-based dyslexia, was offering only the regular first-grade program again, with no remedial help in spoken language or reading. Without intensive practice in small-group and individual instruction, he would continue to experience school failure. In most cases where children with Nicholas's degree of deficit do repeat first grade, they make some progress but not enough to close the gap, so the sense of inadequacy persists. In his case, with a November birthday, Nicholas would subsequently enter second grade two months shy of his ninth birthday, with skills still deficient.

Nicholas's premature birth and low birth weight put him into a high-risk category for developing some learning difficulties. In his small preschool class, with a teacher trained and experienced in child development, his lags and immaturities were more readily recognized as significant. Later, in kindergarten and first grade, the nature of his learning difficulties was not understood.

Because his school could not provide him with an appropriate remedial program, Nicholas entered a nongraded special school for children with dyslexia, where he would receive remedial education in small classes and individual tutorials, until his skills were at a level where he could successfully return to a regular education program. His parents reported several months later that he loved school and was making good progress.

TIM—EARLY IDENTIFICATION OF A CHILD AT RISK FOR DYSLEXIA

Tim was 5 years old when his pediatrician referred him for evaluation, following a kindergarten screening test at his local school. The parents and the doctor were concerned by the school's finding that Tim was not ready for kindergarten and should spend another year in nursery school, and they wanted a fuller assessment of his abilities. The evaluation included parent interviews, standard intelligence and personality measures, and an informal check of his knowledge of letters and numbers. Here is the report of that evaluation, altered only in that test scores have been largely replaced by summaries of the results:

Report of Psychological and Educational Assessment

Selected Background Information from Parents

Tim lives with his parents and older sister. His mother developed diabetes during the eighth month of her pregnancy with Tim and was treated with insulin. Tim was born by C-section, following two days of effort to induce labor. His appearance and behavior upon delivery were normal.

Eating and sleeping are regular, although there seems to be a fair amount of stalling about finally settling down, and he often goes to his parents' bedroom at 4 or 5 in the morning and sleeps on the floor there. Toilet training went easily, and there are no problems of bed-wetting.

Tim's health is generally good. He has had a number of ear infections, but they are decreasing. He is allergic to milk. He was evaluated at Children's Hospital at $2\frac{1}{2}$ for stuttering, and at present he does not articulate well.

He shares when playing with other children, and can also play well by himself. He likes building with Legos and other materials, and using small-size tools. He likes climbing and physical activity in general. He enjoys being outdoors looking for small creatures. He was never interested in *Sesame Street* and does not like to sit and do letters and numbers, or color.

Tim has been reluctant about preschool. At age 3 he attended a program two mornings a week, where he screamed at the beginning and never really was happy to go. Last fall, at age 4 he began nursery school three days a week from 9 to 3. Although he would rather be home with his mother, he became more willing to attend, and was sometimes excited if he had something to contribute.

Tim's father had a problem with stuttering until age 9, and his mother reports that she did not learn to read at school but was taught by her mother.

Observations

I found Tim to be a well-formed, friendly little boy, sturdy though somewhat shorter than average for his age. He related well, enjoyed many of the tasks, and chattered spontaneously from time to time. He sat quietly in his chair through hour-long sessions, calm and attentive, and was able to concentrate for extended periods of time. He was a pleasure to work with, and seemed to be a comfortable and confident child.

Tim appeared slow to respond much of the time, both in taking in new information and also in organizing and expressing a response. His speech is quite immature, with 'r' rarely voiced and 's' substituted for 'sh.' There were also occasional grammatical errors, such as "he have curly hair" and "he like animals," but for the most part he spoke fluently and with good grammar and syntax.

Evaluation

On the Wechsler intelligence test for young children, Tim's scores were in the average range on the three broad IQ measures, and on nine of the twelve component subtests. His lowest scores seemed to result from difficulty in taking in new information, particularly instructions about how to perform an unfamiliar task. On two of the subtests he understood part of the instructions, but not enough to do the tasks correctly without more demonstrations or practice.

On two different tasks of copying geometric figures, Tim scored well on one but below average on the other. The difference between the two tasks was that one set of figures included the drawing of many diagonal lines, including lines in isolation, lines that were part of a figure such as a triangle, and small arrowhead forms.

Tim's drawings of house, tree, and person were awkward, but showed general familiarity with the basic forms and component parts. An exception was the human figure drawing, in which arms and legs were attached to the head, with no neck or torso.

Tim's long-term memory for rote items (letters and numbers) seems particularly weak. Although his mother has worked with him outside of nursery school in an effort to teach him what he has not picked up spontaneously, he still has trouble with the correct naming of written numerals, cannot name most letters of the alphabet, and cannot count to twenty. He can write his name and spell it aloud, but when shown an 'M' in isolation he cannot name it without making reference to the sequence of letters in his name. So he spells his name aloud as he looks at it in written form— 'T-I-M'—then he can name the solitary 'M' written elsewhere. In a task of sentence repetition, which requires immediate auditory recall, he performed well.

Personality testing indicates emotional and social development well within the normal range. Rorschach inkblot responses were particularly impressive in demonstrating clear and organized thinking and perception, and a healthy integration of emotional and cognitive functioning. Issues of closeness to his mother and concern about being strong and competent appear to be well within normal limits and age appropriate.

Summary and Conclusions

Tim is an attractive and appealing little boy with normal intelligence and healthy social and emotional development. He is presently demonstrating a number of developmental lags in areas frequently associated with learning disabilities, although these are not generally apparent until formal schooling has begun. They include problems of motor speech, visual-motor integration in drawing and copying, and memory for the names of letters and numbers. Given that both parents have had difficulties in one or more of these areas, it seems very likely that Tim's current difficulties are hereditary in nature. Because they are being identified at a very early age, and because remedial measures are available today that were not available to his parents when they were growing up, the prognosis for Tim is very good, particularly if he starts receiving extra help in the coming school year.

Because this evaluation has been conducted at the very end of the school year, I have not spoken with his nursery school teachers, so an important source of information is missing. I also have not been in contact with the town special education department, so I do not know what special services are available to children in kindergarten. With these limitations in mind, I will make recommendations based on my work with Tim and the information provided by his parents:

1. Tim would be better served by entering kindergarten in the fall, rather than repeating nursery school. This is based on three factors:
   a. he is intellectually a normal and emotionally solid youngster who is able to sit still and concentrate on material that is appropriate for him;
   b. he is more likely to receive the special services he needs if he is in the public school system; and
   c. if he needs an extra year along the way to solidify his position relative to classmates, he would gain more from repeating the kindergarten or first-grade year than from spending another year in nursery school.
2. Tim should have a speech and language evaluation, to determine whether he could benefit from services in that area.
3. Tim should receive remedial assistance from an occupational therapist who can help him with the skills underlying writing, drawing, and reproducing figures.
4. Tim is at risk for dyslexia once formal reading training begins. To alleviate or prevent this problem from developing, Tim should receive specialized reading help in the coming year. Because he will require more than the usual amount of time to learn letters and numbers, it is important that he begin early with a trained learning disability specialist who is familiar with methods and curriculum for very young children.
5. Tim should have a mainstream classroom placement that offers some individualized programming, which is coordinated with the special services noted in items 2, 3, and 4 above.

Two particular factors in Tim's case marked him as being at high risk for dyslexia: his already evident delay in mastering letter names and sounds, and his mother's difficulty learning to read. Other elements suggesting potential reading difficulties were his various speech and language delays: stuttering, poor articulation, and occasional grammatical errors. His lack of interest in *Sesame Street* suggests he was not "getting it" when he watched the program. His slow pace in taking in new information and in organizing a response might explain his failure to appreciate and enjoy *Sesame Street*, and it would also be a handicap in learning to read at the normal pace of classroom instruction.

Tim's mother contacted me two or three times in the years following the evaluation, to ask a question or update me on his progress. I last spoke with her as Tim was about to enter middle school. Learning to read had indeed proved difficult for him, but he had received remedial assistance from the time he entered kindergarten following the evaluation and was now reading with ease and enjoyment. The remedial help had been gradually reduced so that he was now fully mainstreamed, and he was an industrious student who produced good work. The single remaining problem was in auditory processing; he was still slow at taking in new information, which meant that he often missed some part of directions, instructions, assignments, and the like when they were announced by the teacher. Being a conscientious student, he would usually manage to get the needed information some other way, such as calling a classmate at home later on.

DANIEL—SEVERE DYSLEXIA RESULTING FROM CONGENITAL BRAIN INJURY

I met Daniel Jackson when he was 8 years old. He had suffered serious brain injury at birth. After a normal pregnancy his mother was three weeks overdue, and labor was induced. The birth was very difficult and resulted in skull fractures; in hindsight, he should have been delivered by cesarean section.

Daniel was a healthy child as far as illnesses went, but his development on many fronts was delayed or impaired. All of his language and motor milestones were delayed. He sat at one year, walked at two years. His gross and fine motor coordination were very poor. He learned to ride a tricycle at age 4, and could negotiate stairs well at 6. In addition to poor coordination he was very weak in spatial relations and muscle strength. On a recent plane trip, after several years of failed attempts, he had finally accomplished the task of putting his tray table into the seat back ahead of him, and turning the clasp to lock it in place. He still had difficulty pushing doorbells and elevator buttons. Poor articulation made his speech difficult to understand, and at the age of 8 he was still drooling. On the plus side, he showed many signs of good intelligence in verbal areas: he had a good vocabulary, a good fund of general information, good conceptual understanding, and a sense of humor. He was able to express his ideas well, even though his poor articulation meant that he often might have to repeat himself, and then perhaps not be fully understood.

Daniel lived with his parents and older sister and brother in a large Canadian city. His parents seemed to have come to terms with his slow development, and had found preschool and special school placements for him without too much difficulty. He was a good-natured and compliant boy, although he had some problems with distractibility and short attention span. He had received physical therapy for the past few years at school, but according to the parents had not made much progress.

Mr. and Mrs. Jackson were seeking an evaluation now, when Daniel was 8, because they had recently learned that he was not making progress at school and that the staff did not know how to help him. They found it hard to know what he knew and what he didn't know, because at times he made comments that indicated more attention and problem-solving competence than he generally demonstrated.

From the first, I found Daniel to be an appealing and engaging boy who related directly for the most part. He did a lot of teasing, sometimes as a way to make contact, and sometimes as a defense against being shown as incompetent. I did not find his attention span to be especially short in this one-to-one setting; rather, it seemed that when he was anxious about not being able to do well, he would attempt to joke, or change the subject, or withdraw with an "I don't know."

Daniel presented a number of learning, adjustment, and physical problems. For our purposes here, we will concentrate on his reading difficulties. Testing indicated that he was at early- to mid-first-grade level. He had a small sight vocabulary, recognizing 14 of 50 words on a first-grade list. He knew most consonant sounds, but had little knowledge of vowel sounds. He may have had some isolated concepts: playing at the computer he wrote the word *hat* and then showed me he could change it to *hate* by adding a letter. One of the most enjoyable and encouraging things about Daniel was his real pleasure when he felt successful. His lack of confidence about being able to be successful was a great hindrance, spawning as it did a wide repertoire of avoidance maneuvers.

After this evaluation, I spoke by phone with his principal teacher, to discuss Daniel's need for a program that included direct teaching of letter sounds in a systematic way (in order of difficulty, and not too much new at one time), with rein0 (This is what is often referred to as systematic, multisensory phonics instruction.) We also talked about his fears of being seen as incompetent, his avoidance techniques, and ways to support his efforts so that he could experience frequent success. He was likely to need quite a bit of individual instruction, particularly until he felt more confident. I also recommended to Mr. and Mrs. Jackson that they locate someone in their community who could offer them parent guidance and case management—and for Daniel, that psychotherapy be added to his ongoing speech and physical therapy regimen. There were sufficient funds for any expenses, because there had been a very large insurance settlement following his birth injuries, and the money was placed in trust to be used only for Daniel's care and education.

I was surprised and disappointed when the parents called a year later to arrange a second evaluation. It turned out that no significant changes had been made in any aspect of Daniel's program, either at school or in other domains. Only at this time did I begin to understand that Daniel's parents were unable to pursue any recommendations in a persistent way.

Very handicapped children like Daniel need someone dedicated to finding the care and assistance that most children receive in the normal course of events or with moderate effort, including appropriate schooling, medical attention, and specific therapies. In most cases in which this is undertaken, it constitutes close to a full-time career for the parent. Much as they loved him, Mr. and Mrs. Jackson, with other family circumstances simultaneously demanding and sapping their energies, were unable to do this for Daniel.

The Jacksons did what they could, and I did what I could from a distance, speaking by phone with various teachers and tutors and continuing to see Daniel at yearly intervals until he was 13. During that time his progress in reading was sporadic and minimal. At the evaluation when he was 9, he could identify a few more whole words, and showed no signs of decoding. A year later he was able to sound out a number of three-letter, phonetically regular words such as *cup*, *hit*, and *red*. During the next year he made the greatest progress; in that year he had received intensive, direct phonics training and was able to read both text and isolated words at early second-grade levels. Unfortunately, that reading program was not continued during the next two years, during which his reading ability regressed once more to first-grade level.

I had been talking to Mr. and Mrs. Jackson over the years about the advantages of a residential school program for Daniel, mainly because of the increasing social isolation that was bound to occur in the life of a boy who was very handicapped in his learning, and who could not participate in any physical activity requiring more muscle strength or coordination than taking a walk. They understood and agreed it would someday be necessary, but planned to wait until he was around high school age. At the sixth evaluation, when Daniel was 13 and still a nonreader as well as having no friends or activities outside his immediate family, the parents agreed, though with great trepidation, to launch a school search. A year later, at the age of 14, Daniel received the following letter of acceptance:

Dear Mr. Jackson:

It gives me great pleasure to inform you that you have been accepted in the Academic Program at our school. Welcome to our family. The Admissions Committee reviewed your reports and everyone feels that you will be a good addition to our student body.

We ask a great deal from our students. We believe that with guidance and family support, you will study hard, make friends, and become more independent.

Congratulations on your acceptance. We are happy that you are going to be with us in July.

Fondly,
Mrs. Jane Smith
Director of Admissions

Daniel did very well at the residential school. Six years later he graduated from the high school program, with reading skills at fourth-grade level and reading comprehension at seventh-grade level. He had friends and was an integral member of an active and supportive community. Following graduation he stayed on in a postgraduate program dedicated to independent living skills and work experience.

Daniel's story contains a number of important lessons. The first and most encouraging is that it is never too late to learn to read; and that almost everyone could learn to read at a functional level as long as they had a structured setting in which to learn, and a systematic instructional program that was appropriate to their particular constellation of skills and deficiencies. The second lesson is that for children with handicaps that will affect learning to read, the sooner they can learn underlying subskills (such as awareness of word segments, and the ability to recite the alphabet and recognize the letters in print), the better prepared they will be when true reading instruction begins. (This is not to be confused with the notion of teaching nondyslexic children to read when they are very young, a practice that I believe is rarely in the best interests of the child.)

The third lesson of Daniel's story is that significant delay in learning to read comfortably and efficiently has far-reaching deleterious effects. In some respects, Daniel's story is reminiscent of Bill's difficulties, with Daniel's being far more serious. Daniel's diminishing self-esteem had to do with multiple disabilities, not just reading; Bill's reading, though deficient, was functional through much of his boyhood as well as later, allowing him to keep pace with much that went on in his ever-widening world. Daniel's world was limited in so many ways, and his inability to read until mid-adolescence deprived him of a very wide window for broadening his outlook, as well as for expanding his vocabulary, information base, and conceptual abilities.

The cases in this chapter span a range of ages, personal styles, severity, and types of problems, but one thing they have in common is the lack of preparedness in their schools either to recognize the existence of their reading difficulty, or to know how to understand and respond to the problem. In some instances the classroom teachers did not know that the children were having a problem with reading: Sally's teacher didn't know that Sally was misreading so many words or taking such a long time with her homework; Robert's teachers didn't know he was error-prone and avoiding reading as much as possible; Eileen's teachers didn't know she had a reading problem until she went to her mother in eighth grade. Nicholas's teachers knew he had trouble reading, but believed another year in first grade would solve things by allowing him to catch up developmentally. Similarly, the kindergarten teachers who screened Tim wanted him to spend another year in nursery school. Daniel's teachers didn't understand his need to learn the code.

The lack of appropriate response to the children was not due to their having poor teachers. The great majority of those I met impressed me as intelligent, conscientious, concerned individuals whose professional training did not include understanding the nature of reading and its difficulties. The next chapter considers why this is the case and what can be done about it.

▶ 7

Teaching Everyone to Read

In the previous chapters we have examined the reading process, looking at how children learn to read and at the impediments they may encounter. We have sampled the stories of a number of people to whom reading did not come easily. The focus has been on individuals, and on the unique set of circumstances that resulted in their reading difficulty. But for many learners, a common and major source of difficulty has been the failure of their schools to recognize their deficiencies and provide the necessary interventions that would help overcome them. As a prominent recent study, *Preventing Reading Difficulties in Young Children*, notes, "The majority of reading problems faced by today's adolescents and adults are the result of problems that might have been avoided or resolved in their early childhood years" (Snow, Burns, & Griffin, 1998, p. 5).

To understand better some of the factors interfering with learning to read in the early school years, we shift in this chapter to a broader perspective. We begin by reviewing the history of reading instruction in this country, with particular attention to the prominent concerns over if, when, and how to teach phonics. Next we take stock of where we are and what we know today about teaching reading to all children, including those with any degree of dyslexia or dyslexia-like weaknesses.

Finally, in light of past history and current knowledge we recommend a perspective on reading instruction to assist teachers, reading specialists, and school administrators in designing programs that will help many more children learn to read well in the early grades, and provide appropriate intensive instruction for the few who need that.

THE SWINGING PENDULUM: A BRIEF HISTORY OF INSTRUCTION IN BEGINNING READING

The field of education is well known for wide pendulum swings in its teaching philosophy and methods, particularly in reading and math. In reading, the last twenty years or so have seen the development of the Whole Language Movement, an approach to reading instruction that emphasizes meaning and pleasure in reading and pays scant attention to learning the phonics code. This approach has had a great impact on teacher training and on the way many children have been taught to read. Although new in the last quarter century, whole language nonetheless reflects and repeats attitudes about human nature, democracy, and social circumstances that have been intrinsic to arguments in this country about how to teach reading for more than one hundred and fifty years. We start with early times in this country, when there appears to have been no dispute about how to teach children to read.

Noah Webster and Horace Mann

Our anchoring point in this brief history of teaching reading in America is Noah Webster (1758–1843), who came of age during the Revolutionary War, attending Yale from 1774 to 1778. Like later educators, he was a dedicated patriot and deeply interested in education and its role in establishing and preserving democratic principles in the new nation. An activist and reformer, he was eager to establish an American English language, as well as to improve educational practice by raising standards and making schooling accessible to all, rich or poor. Best known as the founding father of the American dictionary, he also wrote a spelling book that ultimately sold more than a hundred million copies—an American best-seller, second only to the Bible. Webster saw no need for reform in the teaching of reading. He wrote reading books that followed the traditional teaching method in England, presenting first the alphabet letters, then syllables (ab, eb, ob, ba, be, bo, and so on), and then short words in isolation and in brief passages, all presented for rote learning. This was the composition of primers in America for many years; when the student had mastered the primer book he moved on to other texts, and received little additional instruction in reading from that point on (Smith, 1965).

Horace Mann (1796–1859) was among the earliest and most eloquent Americans to champion the use of whole words, rather than letters and syllables, as the first items to be identified in learning to read. This approach was first advocated by Friedrich Gedike, a German schoolteacher who put his ideas in writing in 1779 (Balmuth, 1982, pp. 184–185). Gedike reasoned that children would find meaning, and therefore also pleasure, in learning to recognize whole words rather than parts of words, and so whole words should be presented before phonics instruction. He recommended that after children learned to recognize a whole word, they should be helped to analyze it according to the sounds that its letters made, and then put the sounds together so as to reconstruct the whole word. This process of analyzing and then synthesizing words was to be followed up with more systematic phonics instruction. Gedike thus recognized, in the task of learning to read, the three stages of what later became Heinz Werner's orthogenetic principle:

- that the first recognition (or awareness or perception or knowledge) comes holistically in a global, undifferentiated way;
- that this is followed by an analysis of the parts; and
- that the parts can then be perceived in relation to each other and also as constituting the whole.

This is a good place to clarify an important distinction made about teaching phonics. When letter sounds are taught as a focus in and of themselves, we speak of direct, explicit, or systematic instruction in phonics. When letter sounds receive attention only as elements in whole words that the child comes upon, we describe it as indirect, incidental, or opportunistic phonics instruction. An important difference among reading instruction programs is the extent to which they include, if at all, direct instruction in phonics.

Mann was an enthusiastic proponent of Gedike's idea that children's reading experience should be tied to meaning rather than rote learning of symbols. Mann toured Europe in 1843, and visits to classrooms using this approach strengthened his views on the matter. However, he was apparently unaware that Gedike's method did include direct phonics instruction after introducing whole words and the analysis/synthesis of those words. When Mann returned to America from his European visit, he devoted much of his energy to advancing his own understanding of this whole word approach, and he was well situated to disseminate his ideas widely.

Like Webster, Mann's interest in education was driven by strong patriotic feelings and humanitarian concerns. He served in the Massachusetts legislature for ten years, advancing to the post of Senate president. He was instrumental in the legislature's decision to establish the Massachusetts Board of Education, and in 1837 he left the legislature to become the first secretary and administrative director of that body. He believed fervently in public education as the vehicle for creating and maintaining a democratic society, and his views on education, expressed in his annual reports to the board of education, were well publicized and evoked both high praise and strong criticism. Mann's critics correctly pointed out that he had misunderstood the reading system he observed in Europe, but in addition there were intense rhetorical barrages from each side condemning the wrongheadedness of the other. Mann's battles with his critics about reading are of interest to us for two reasons: First, the arguments about whole word versus phonics raised questions still used in contemporary debates; for example, are the exceptions to "regular" spellings of words so great as to make learning letter and syllable sounds useless? Second, Mann's emotional championing of whole words brought political philosophy into the debate, so that whole word and later whole language approaches were frequently cast as liberal and enlightened, whereas teaching phonics was characterized as conservative, rigid, and even inhumane. In one lecture Mann referred to letters as "skeleton-shaped, bloodless, ghostly apparitions," stating "hence it is no wonder that the children look and feel so deathlike, when compelled to face them" (cited in Balmuth, 1982).

The Progressive Education Movement

Mann's endorsement of whole word teaching and his aversion to direct phonics instruction had growing influence for many years. Among others, prominent educators like John Dewey (1859–1952) found the whole word method congenial to their major educational mission, the advancement of progressive education. A central principle of progressive education was that children naturally develop skills for schoolwork including reading, and that they should not be forced into academic activities for which they are not yet physically, mentally, or emotionally ready. The ideas promoted by progressive education about the nature of children and their capacities at various ages, along with the firm commitment to following the child's interests rather than a prestructured curriculum, had a long-lasting effect on reading instruction that went beyond the whole word approach.

The progressive education movement was very successful in heightening awareness that children are not miniature adults, that each child deserves the care and attention appropriate to his current developmental level, and that the child's active involvement in his own education is one of the most powerful keys to learning. At the same time, it also generated a number of specific directives for reading instruction that, it is now apparent, have no scientific basis and work to the detriment of many children. Among these were the withholding of letter names when teaching letter sounds (so that the children would not be confused), and delaying the teaching of reading altogether until the child was 8 years old or showed an interest in reading (Balmuth, 1982, pp. 194–196).

For practical purposes we can identify the 1840s as the beginning of the dichotomized battle between adherents of code-based (phonics) and meaning-based (whole word) approaches to learning to read, which has continued to the present day. Chall (1983, p. 133) notes that by 1920, although direct phonics instruction was still widely practiced in schools, whole word was the "in" theoretical approach. And from about 1930 to the early 1960s, most textbooks for teachers and publishers' reading programs for children were recommending that direct phonics instruction be avoided (Chall, 1983, pp. 13–15).

Back to Phonics

The shift that occurred in the 1960s was precipitated largely by the 1955 publication of Rudolf Flesch's book, *Why Johnny Can't Read*, which dominated best-seller lists for more than thirty weeks, and was widely reported on and serialized in the popular press. Flesch urged a wholesale return to teaching phonics first. In dramatic language, he roundly condemned the whole word method as a form of animal training rather than teaching, a system that expected children to learn to recognize whole words by rote training, instead of providing them the tools inherent in phonics teaching. Like others before and after him, Flesch claimed that his stance on the reading question was consonant with democratic ideals that rely on high-quality education in the public schools. He declared that the whole word method worked for the elite, who could intuit the alphabetic nature of print, but that not teaching phonics to those who did not catch on spontaneously was depriving them of equal opportunity, and therefore of access to the American Dream (Flesch, 1955, pp. 126–132).

Why Johnny Can't Read stirred up a great deal of public interest and general debate. Whereas the press reacted favorably, the educational establishment largely rejected Flesch's arguments, but the nature of the argument had changed. This time, both sides of the debate now claimed validity for their respective positions on scientific grounds, frequently citing the same piece of research to justify their opposing interpretations. One important outcome of this new phase of debate was the formation in 1959 of a special committee on research in reading. Spurred on by the interest of the public, the bitterness of the debate, and the invocation of science in the reading controversy, the committee gathered for a three-day conference at Syracuse University. During the conference, the experts identified important variables to be studied in future research. These were the seeds that grew into a large project sponsored by the U.S. Office of Education: the Cooperative Research Program in First-Grade Reading Instruction, conducted between 1964 and 1967.

Jeanne Chall, professor of education at Harvard and a seasoned reading expert, was one of the conference participants at Syracuse in 1959, and she developed another project around the same time. In 1961 she applied to the Carnegie Corporation for support of a study to carry out a critical analysis of *existing* research comparing different approaches to beginning reading. Chall's aims were to discover what was already known from prior studies, point out specific gaps in knowledge, and help future experimenters design more meaningful research (Chall, 1983, p. 5). She conducted her study from 1962 to 1965, and in 1967 her findings reached the general public in what has become a classic work, *Learning to Read: The Great Debate*. It was a best-seller at the time of its original publication, and has since been updated and reissued twice, in 1983 and again in 1996.

After reviewing hundreds of studies, Chall found that most of them seemed to have been undertaken to support a strongly held belief about a method or practice rather than to replicate or add to previous studies. In addition, she found that researchers were heavily influenced by philosophical assumptions and by the social problems of their time, both in selecting topics of study and in drawing conclusions and making recommendations (Chall, 1983, pp. 88–89). Her recognition of these weaknesses has had a tremendous positive influence on future research.

The most important result of Chall's study was the finding that code-emphasis programs produced better results than meaning-emphasis programs. This finding was confirmed in several other large-scale studies, including the government's Cooperative Research Program in First-Grade Reading Instruction, which was carried out during the same period. Based on these research findings and widespread publicity about them, by the 1970s publishers began including more phonics activities in their reading instructional materials, and phonics teaching began to reappear in many classrooms across the country. The 1983 reissue of *The Great Debate* opens with an "Update" covering what had transpired in reading instruction in the intervening years; Chall wrote, "Beginning with the 1970s, the importance of phonics teaching seemed to have become generally accepted, and the research question turned to which kind of phonics was the more effective" (Chall, 1983, p. 12). (However, Chall did note that in spite of the general acceptance of her findings, the educators in teacher training programs were resistant to them, a reaction that was to be seen again several years later following Adams's [1990] study.) Upon reviewing the studies carried out between the 1967 and 1983 publications, Chall found indications of an advantage for direct phonics instruction (Chall, 1983, p. 16). Two years later, the authors of *Becoming a Nation of Readers*—a report based on research of the National Commission on Reading—came to the same conclusion.

In the late 1960s through the 1970s, the pendulum of reading instruction swung back to a greater emphasis on direct phonics instruction. It appeared that educational practice was turning in the direction of the research findings. Who could have dreamed that in the next ten to fifteen years it would swing back and forth yet again, first in the direction of diminishing phonics instruction (and in some instances shunning it altogether), and then once again back toward phonics?

The Whole Language Movement

Whole language is the name given to the most recent, late-twentieth-century version of teaching reading via whole word and meaning-emphasis instruction. Its adherents want to offer children intellectually challenging literature to read, instead of sterile "Dick and Jane" stories or boring phonics drills. The most extreme proponents of whole language are averse to any kind of drill, including single whole words as well as phonemes or syllables. These adherents take to heart Frank Smith's pronouncement: the idea "that learning requires effort is another myth," as he states in his book, *Insult to Intelligence* (cited in Lemann, 1997).

In fact, the initial impetus to the Whole Language Movement seems to have been Frank Smith's 1971 publication, *Understanding Reading*, although the long swing of the pendulum away from phonics did not become evident until the mid-1980s. By that time, Smith had been joined by Kenneth Goodman as a leading spokesman for whole language, and publishers' instruction materials and teacher training programs were heavily committed to the whole language approach. A 1987 survey of forty-three texts used to train teachers of reading found that *none* of them advocated systematic phonics instruction and only nine even indicated that there was any debate on the matter (Levine, 1994).

The major focus of whole language proponents is the importance of having children read for meaning and enjoyment, but they also promote other principles that grew out of the progressive education movement. These include creating child-centered classrooms, combining the teaching of reading and writing, and empowering teachers to free themselves from restrictive curriculum requirements imposed from above. The emphasis on meaning and the child-centered classroom are clear echoes from previous times, and once again evoke an image of releasing children from dreary and useless drudgery, and bringing them to joyful understanding and intellectual development. The wish to empower teachers reflects the widespread dissatisfaction of many educators, who feel that central administrative officers are increasing their authority over the choice of classroom materials and methods. Some whole language advocates also employ a political argument: teaching phonics, they say, is detrimental to low-income and other disadvantaged children in their efforts to learn to read. Ironically, this appeal to democratic principles is exactly the opposite of Flesch's 1955 claim, that whole word instruction is antidemocratic.

What *is* totally new in whole language theory is the notion that learning to read is as natural a process as learning to speak, and that children will learn to read without specific instruction in the skills of reading if they are immersed in reading (as in infancy they were immersed in spoken language). The strongly held belief is that if children are read to, and if their environment is adequately supplied with simple, attractive text, they will pick up on their own what they need to know in order to read. A child who comes upon an unfamiliar word is encouraged to skip it, or guess, using context in order to arrive at meaning. In some instances children are specifically told "Don't sound it out" (Levine, 1994).

Whole language leaders Frank Smith and Kenneth Goodman have made dramatic, peremptory statements about the nature of reading. Goodman believes that accuracy is not an essential goal of reading, and has in fact characterized reading as a "psycholinguistic guessing game" (Goodman, 1967). In a similar vein Smith explained to a journalist that "to the fluent reader the alphabetic principle is completely irrelevant" (Levine, 1994). These beliefs are at the heart of any debate between whole language and phonics adherents. Phonics adherents have no argument with the Whole Language Movement's stress on good literature and meaningful texts for children, although polarization of the two camps has led to the mistaken belief in some quarters that all phonics adherents oppose early introduction of literature and other meaningful text and that all whole language proponents are opposed to any kind of phonics training.

One way to understand the thinking of whole language adherents is to recall Heinz Werner's orthogenetic principle as it applies to reading. Stage I involves global, impressionistic perception of the whole (word). Stage II is more concerned with analysis of the parts that make up the whole. At Stage III the whole word is once again the main focus, but this time the whole is recognized in an integrated way with an awareness of the parts and how they relate to each other and to the whole. The whole language approach, in which children are asked to guess at, rather than decode, an unfamiliar word, fails to give Stage II its proper place in the development of reading competency. If the implicit assumption is that the children will learn the grapheme-phoneme pairs on their own, without direct instruction, teachers using this approach are at high risk for hearing children read who don't know the code thoroughly but whose whole word recognition and intelligent guessing make it seem that they do. In other words, teachers can hear Stage I reading and believe it is actually Stage III reading.

The modern battle between whole language and phonics adherents has been as bitter and divisive as any stirred up by Horace Mann's pressing for change to whole word and meaning, or Rudolf Flesch's demanding a return to phonics. For example, at a meeting of the International Reading Association, a leading proponent of whole language characterized a major researcher who supports phonics instruction as a vampire threatening the literacy of American youth (Levine, 1994).

Back to Phonics Again

In the mid-1990s the pendulum began to swing back toward phonics once again. In retrospect, several significant events probably contributed to the shift:

1. In 1986 the U.S. Office of Education sponsored a study carried out by Marilyn Jager Adams, which reviewed what was then known about basic processes and instruction practices in word and letter identification and early reading. Adams's work, published in 1990 as *Beginning to Read: Thinking and Learning about Print*, picked up where Chall's work had left off. When Chall did her work she was dealing largely with small studies designed to answer practical, "local" questions such as "Which program worked best?" Adams was able to take into account new theoretical understanding and more sophisticated and reliable research information than had been available to Chall. Adams's work was praised as a highly comprehensive and readable reference work on beginning reading instruction, widely recommended and frequently referred to by reading specialists and researchers. It reached the conclusion that direct, early teaching of phonics is a critical element in learning to read.

(As with Chall's report, the generally enthusiastic response to Adams's work was not shared among those who trained teachers. Two professors of education, who sat on the advisory panel that reviewed Adams's work before publication, saw the need to offer an Afterword at the end of Adams's book, which presses the basic whole language belief. The Afterword includes the following statement about children in print-rich environments: "Because the learning is so joyful and natural, the development of specific skills may not be in evidence. Nevertheless, the skills, including phonics, are there" [Adams, 1990, p. 428]. In other words, the statement claims that if the children are happy and involved, phonics will come without explicit instruction. Even if there is no evidence that they are learning the code, we know in our hearts that they must be learning it.)

2. In 1985 Congress passed legislation that enabled the National Institute of Child Health and Human Development (NICHD) to improve the quality of reading research by conducting long-term, prospective, longitudinal, and multidisciplinary research. Researchers in more than twenty centers

around the country have been carrying out a number of studies, the results of which are released as information is collated and analyzed. G. Reid Lyon has been the director of research programs in learning disabilities since 1991, and he reports regularly through scholarly publications, as well as testifies before a number of concerned congressional committees. For example, his statement to the U.S. Senate Committee on Labor and Human Resources in April 1998, entitled *Overview of Reading and Literacy Initiatives*, provides a comprehensive review of the current state of knowledge (Lyon, April 1998). It explains the nature of reading difficulties and stresses the importance of early, direct teaching of phonics. Lyon's report is organized around three questions:

How Do Children Learn to Read?

Why Do Some Children (and Adults) Have Difficulties Learning to Read?

How Can We Help Children Learn to Read?

3. In 1993 and 1996, the reading scores of California students dropped precipitously on a national test administered in every state and territory. California students had previously done very well on these tests, and residents were stunned to find their state ranking fifth from the bottom in 1993 and second from the bottom in 1996. In the late 1980s, California had shifted dramatically toward whole language instruction; much of the blame for the drop in scores was placed on the resulting move away from phonics instruction. The California scores had an effect similar to the 1955 publication of *Why Johnny Can't Read:* the news spread rapidly, and in the fall of 1997 a spate of programs and articles appeared throughout the country, including TV shows, newspaper articles, and articles in widely read magazines such as *Time* and *Newsweek*. By this time the results of NICHD research as well as Adams's work were available, and the media reports often included interviews with researchers who articulated not only the importance of phonics but the evidence accumulated to support that position.

4. In the spring of 1998, a committee established by the National Academy of Sciences at the request of the U.S. Department of Education and the U.S. Department of Health and Human Services published a report entitled *Preventing Reading Difficulties in Young Children* (Snow, Burns, & Griffin, 1998). The committee's charge was to conduct a study of the effectiveness of interventions for young children at risk of having problems learning to read. However, its review and investigation extended to the instruction of all children learning to read. Because this committee included professors of education formerly on record as minimizing the importance of teaching phonics, its conclusions about the need for phonics instruction may carry more weight with teacher training institutions than prior studies.

As this is written, in the spring of 1999, the pendulum has definitely swung back toward a general belief that learning phonics is important, and perhaps toward acceptance of the importance of direct instruction of phonics. For a number of years teachers have been seeking out postgraduate courses to learn about teaching phonics, and parents have gone to outside tutors and franchised academic centers to get help in reading for their children. The business world stepped in with phonics programs that can be bought in stores or by mail order, many of them in the form of computer software. In recent years the California legislature mandated phonics training in statewide in-service courses for teachers. Teacher training programs at colleges and universities seem to be shifting as well, with a number of them trying to revise their reading education programs as quickly as possible. Given the consistent results of studies since Chall's 1967 *Learning to Read: The Great Debate*, and the continuing longitudinal research at NICHD, perhaps we will not see the pendulum swing so far or so soon, at least where reading is concerned.

Chall is less sanguine about the permanency of the return to phonics instruction. She attributes the swinging pendulum in part to the appeal of fad and fashion, and the interest in something new. As people swing from code to meaning emphasis and back again, they are largely unaware that they are not switching to something new, but to a recent version of something old. After her experience in seeing whole language dominate so soon on the heels of her 1967 study and the return to phonics for a time in the 1970s, who can blame her for this pessimistic statement? ". . . I cannot be completely joyful about the present return to explicit teaching of skills and phonics. If we take our own history seriously, we can expect the return of a whole-language type method even if under a new label, in about 10 or 15 years" (Chall, 1997, p. 261). In any event, even with the full support of teacher training programs, it will take time to train a new generation of classroom teachers, retrain current teachers, and organize reading programs within schools so that students at all levels will receive reading instruction appropriate to their skills and attentive to their deficiencies.

Before leaving the history of the swinging pendulum, it will be helpful to clarify a common misunderstanding. Noah Webster believed that the way to learn the basic elements of the language, both letters and syllables, was by rote memory and all at once, with meaningful text withheld until the letters and sounds were learned. That is not how phonics is presented today. When reading experts recommend teaching phonics early and explicitly, they are not suggesting it be to the exclusion of other reading matter. In all stages of early reading instruction children are dealing with phonics, isolated words, and texts. Some unfamiliar words and sounds not yet learned may be included in the text, but there is an effort to "control" vocabulary so that the children are practicing sounds they have already learned. The goal is always to keep children engaged in their work through enjoyment of their own success, or the stimulating material, and as much as possible both of these. Unfortunately, many of those opposing direct teaching of phonics believe that to do so is to engage in old-fashioned "drill and kill" methods.

WHAT WE KNOW TODAY ABOUT PROMOTING READING ACQUISITION

In the previous section on the history of reading instruction the focus was on teaching phonics. We now turn to other important findings and conclusions drawn from recent research, comprehensive reviews of previous research, and educational practice.

From Research

Phonemic Awareness
Toward the end of Chapter 2 we mentioned Mr. Green, who had difficulty isolating the last sound in the word *equipment*. In the last twenty years or so, there has been intense interest in the role of phonemic awareness among reading researchers and clinicians. Many dyslexic children are weak in phonemic awareness; that is, they do not discriminate, or discriminate easily, the individual phonemes that constitute the sounds in a word. Those to whom this skill does not come easily or intuitively must learn it by example, imitation, and practice. There is already evidence that starting to teach phonemic awareness in kindergarten has good results; that is, the children learn the skill, and they also make better progress when reading instruction is introduced later on (Torgesen, 1997). Studies are currently under way, examining how preschoolers respond to instruction in phonemic awareness. We will look at phonemic awareness in more detail in Chapter 8.

Early Intervention
There is strong evidence that children are greatly helped when their reading difficulties are identified early and they are given prompt direct instruction. Currently few children are identified as having reading disabilities before third grade, but with appropriate training, teachers could spot children at risk in kindergarten or first grade.

Reading Readiness and Developmental Delays
A corollary to the principle of early intervention is the need to reconsider our long-standing concepts of reading readiness

and developmental delay. Although some children do teach themselves to read at an early age and some learn later, it is neither helpful nor accurate to think of reading as a developmental milestone that all children will come to in their own time. This does not mean that children who are learning more slowly should be pushed to keep up with some predetermined standard. It does mean that they should not be left to flounder, nor allowed to avoid reading as long as possible.

Accuracy and Automaticity

Research has demonstrated that the whole language method of instructing children to use context and to guess at unfamiliar words results in more cases of reading disability than teaching them to use decoding (Lyon, March 1998). A major fallacy of the whole language movement is the belief that good readers skim text, taking in only as much detail as is necessary to comprehend the text. In fact, the research indicates that good readers do not "sample" the text, but rather see every letter and punctuation mark on the page. Their high level of accuracy is what ultimately makes possible fluency and automaticity in reading (Adams, 1990).

Regular Spellings

This term refers to those words that are pronounced according to the most common sound-symbol, or sound-spelling, patterns in the language. Early in the teaching of phonics, children are taught the most common short vowel sounds, as they occur in such words as *can, met, fib, hop,* and *nut.* (Teachers use a shorthand name for these words, referring to them as c-v-c words, meaning that they consist of three letters that appear in the order of consonant-vowel-consonant. Children are also taught somewhat complex regular spellings, such as '_ight' words (*light, might, fright,* and so on) and c-v-c-e words (*fame, site, note, tune*). These spelling patterns, which appear with high frequency in reading matter, with consistent and predictable pronunciations, are what allowed you to read that nonsense word in Chapter 2, *sentinasculate.* Yet those opposed to phonics instruction argue that there are so many irregular spellings in the English language that teaching phonics is pointless. Modern research has established that regular spellings far outnumber irregular (Moats, 1995a), and that children are very much helped in learning to read when their first exposures are to regularly spelled words.

In addition to the lessons learned from research and clinical practice in the area of reading disability, there are a number of general instructional principles that are particularly useful in teaching children with reading difficulties.

From Educational Practice

Sequence, Simultaneity, and Spiraling

All three terms refer to the *timing* of instruction. *Sequence* has to do with the order in which new material is presented, and as common sense tells us, there is a progression from the easy to the difficult. What constitutes "easy" is determined as much as possible by what children find easier. Consonants are easier than vowels, initial consonants in words are easier than final consonants and much easier than consonants in the middle of a word, and so on. Simple, high-frequency words that have great meaning to small children are easier to remember than individual letters and sounds. Text that is familiar or accompanied by pictures is easier than straight text on unfamiliar topics. The fact that sequential presentation of material is very important does not mean that it has to be rigid. There will always be children who learn things "out of order," who find some things difficult that most children find easy.

Simultaneity refers to the fact that different aspects of beginning reading are being presented to the children simultaneously. They will be learning new whole words in a global (Stage I) manner at the same time that they are learning phonics in a systematic, analytic manner. They may be dictating their own stories and reading them back, or they may be reading from large "experience charts" that the teacher writes on an easel at the front of the classroom. And they may be reading the short, simple texts of educational publishers or Dr. Seuss.

Spiraling is the educational practice of going back from time to time to review and reinforce earlier instruction, and also to present previously taught material in a more complex way to students who are now older and capable of broader and deeper understanding. With regard to reading instruction, it is important to review previously learned phonics elements and sight words periodically. Spiraling is an opportunity for teachers to identify weaknesses in individual students who did not learn the first time or who learned and subsequently forgot.

Slower Pace

Because children with dyslexia are less skilled in one or more of the perceptual and memory skills required for word identification, they need more than the ordinary number of exposures and practice sessions in order to recognize and remember the various elements of the code. These children will proceed more slowly through the curriculum for learning the elements, reviewing, and practicing, before moving on to new material. One of the creative tasks of teaching is finding new and fresh ways of presenting the same basic elements over and over again, in different contexts and formats.

Tasks Broken Down into Smaller Segments

A corollary to slowing the pace is breaking up large units of material into smaller chunks. Large is a relative term here. For example, it may involve something as small as a two-syllable word; if a child doesn't recognize the word, or is unable to sound out and hold in mind the various elements, the teacher may cover up part of the word and encourage the child to focus on a smaller part. Or a student having trouble understanding the content of a chapter she is reading might be encouraged to take it one paragraph at a time. She might read a paragraph aloud or silently, and then discuss that material with a teacher or fellow student to clarify the meaning before moving on.

Linguistic Rules and Analysis to Supplement Perception and Memory

A number of structural features of words assist the reader in word identification. For example, there are rules governing how to break words into syllables, making it easier to sound out multisyllabic words. Learning to analyze words according to root, prefix, and suffix facilitates word identification by making it easier to recognize word segments beyond the phoneme and syllable level.

To a great extent, these findings and conclusions are the outcome of a series of clinical observations and research studies that began with the objective of discovering the specific weaknesses underlying dyslexia and how to overcome them. As weaknesses associated with dyslexia became apparent, some researchers turned their attention to the general population to see if the same weaknesses were also associated with poor performance in that broader group of children. This is in large measure the case. For many years, we believed that the reading difficulties of children diagnosed as dyslexic were categorically different from the reading difficulties of other children who were given extra help at school, often in what was called a "remedial reading program." It is now apparent that the major differences among children who have difficulty with word identification (decoding or whole word recognition) are differences of degree rather than type.

This process of discovery is similar to advances in other fields, including medicine and mental health, in which the study of abnormal conditions yields greater understanding of normal function. This in turn often leads to recognition that there is a steady progression from normal to abnormal levels, with only a somewhat arbitrary cutoff point separating the two. And if the normal and abnormal are on the same continuum, we have now learned to ask whether there are preventive measures that will reduce the incidence or severity of abnormal cases. Finding and implementing preventive measures is essentially a public health approach to disease control, one that has much to offer when applied to the (nondisease) dyslexia spectrum and the goal of solid reading acquisition.

A PUBLIC HEALTH APPROACH TO ENHANCING READING ACQUISITION

Four aspects of a public health approach are particularly relevant to preventing reading difficulties: *inevitability, invisibility, preventive measures,* and *need for regular monitoring.* We will look at them as they apply both to a familiar health risk—heart disease—and to reading problems. For the most part we will be using the term *reading disabilities* so as to include both dyslexia (difficulty with word identification) and reading difficulties that more directly affect comprehension. The term *dyslexia-type difficulties* will be used to refer to those very mild cases within the range or on the border of normal functioning.

Inevitability

In regard to both heart disease and reading disabilities, we know that some individuals will be born with biological characteristics that create a high risk, and in some cases a certainty, of developing the condition. In addition, environmental circumstances may create added risk. For heart disease, poor diet and lack of exercise are adverse factors, whereas reading disabilities are adversely affected by home environments that do not promote experience with print and school programs that fail to provide appropriate instruction. Unlike some other disabling conditions and diseases, such as tuberculosis or polio, there is no absolute cure for either heart disease or reading disabilities although effective treatments are available for both. Therefore, we know that at some point individuals will come to the attention of professionals as requiring assessment and treatment. It is best when professionals are prepared to welcome and help them, rather than being surprised and disappointed by these instances of "failure." In the case of reading disabilities, it will be very helpful when there is broad understanding that the condition develops from circumstances beyond personal control, and does not signal lack of intelligence or motivation.

Invisibility

In both heart disease and reading disabilities, the underlying causative agents are present but "silent" until the first signs of failure occur. Heart disease is not likely to be uncovered until late into adult life. A reading disability, under the best of circumstances, will not be discovered until a child enters formal schooling, and in today's world it is rarely noted before late third grade, most frequently going undiagnosed altogether. In this matter, there is a significant difference between heart disease and reading disabilities. When heart disease interferes with functioning, there are manifest symptoms (heart attack, chest pain) that signal the presence of the disease. Until teachers and parents have a better understanding of reading disabilities, they will remain invisible long beyond the time when they have begun to have a deleterious effect on the child's competence and confidence.

Preventive Measures

In the last fifty years great progress has been made in identifying risk factors for heart disease, along with methods for eliminating or ameliorating them. Smoking, high blood pressure, poor diet, and lack of exercise are major contributors to elevated cholesterol levels and clogged arteries, and highly effective treatment is available through medication and behavior change. Because of the invisibility of heart disease, no one can say for certain who is a candidate for the illness, and so the public at large has been encouraged to make health-enhancing choices in their daily lives: quit or don't start smoking, eat a heart-healthy diet, get adequate general and aerobic exercise, and keep your cholesterol levels and blood pressure within a healthy range (through medication if necessary).

At home, preventive measures for reading disabilities begin in infancy and continue through early childhood. As prevention of heart disease depends on proper diet and exercise, prevention of reading disabilities is linked to a home environment rich in stimulating and pleasurable language activity. The importance of adults reading to children is widely recognized, and there are other play activities and parent-child interactions that enhance the development of a child's language capabilities. These are described in Chapter 8. Children who arrive at kindergarten and first grade without this prior introduction to language and print activities have to play catchup from the first day, and are at higher risk for difficulties in learning to read.

At school, the most recently developed preventive measure for dyslexia is phonemic awareness training, which can be presented as a regular part of the curriculum for classroom groups in kindergarten and perhaps preschool. Children who cannot easily distinguish the separate sound elements of a word such as *cat* are going to have significant difficulty sounding out words when formal reading instruction begins in first grade. As with many other skills, what is not grasped intuitively can be learned by consciousness raising and practice. Because the games and play activities that have been developed for phonemic awareness training are appealing to children of all ability levels, those at high risk do not initially have to be identified or singled out for special training, and those not at risk will enjoy the activities whether or not they need them for therapeutic benefit. This particular preventive measure has great added value as a diagnostic tool, because it will automatically bring to light those children who continue to have difficulty with the task in spite of the training they have received.

Regular Monitoring

There is considerable public awareness about symptoms and risk factors in heart disease, and a large part of the general adult population is monitored through routine medical checkups. Many people recognize the significance of chest pain and shortness of breath and know they need to consult a doctor. Individuals known to have heart disease or to be at high risk can be followed closely with blood tests, stress tests, and other diagnostic procedures, and for those whose disease is not well controlled or whose risk appears to be increasing, there are prevention and rehabilitation programs available through hospital and clinic cardiology departments. To put it another way, the public is aware of the existence and symptomatology of the disease, and the medical community is prepared to assess, treat, and intervene proactively with preventive measures.

For both the detection and prevention of dyslexia and dyslexia-type reading difficulties, children's skills should be checked at regular intervals until it is established that they are accurate and efficient readers. As we saw in the cases presented in Chapter 6, failure to monitor the level of technical reading skill each child has reached is a critical weakness in elementary grades and beyond. In the early primary grades, a child's difficulties in such skills as phonemic awareness, learning of the code, whole word recognition, and smooth reading of texts can be detected by a classroom teacher or reading specialist using a brief, easily administered skill survey (for an example, see Torgesen, Wagner, & Rashotte, 1999). It is important for children in later grades to be checked as well, for there are a number who do well in learning the code but have trouble with accuracy when they read dense or complex text. Older children with reading weaknesses can be readily identified if each student reads aloud in class as part of a lesson, or in private for a reading screening. (Traditional standardized reading tests are not a substitute for students reading aloud before a teacher. Many poor readers who are slow or inaccurate can do reasonably well on the brief texts of standardized group reading tests, making use of context and previous knowledge.)

We have used the model of public health as a metaphor and framework for tackling the problem of reading disability. However, G. Reid Lyon, Chief of the Child Development and Behavior Branch of the National Institute of Child Health and Human Development, has argued that difficulty learning to read is *in fact* a public health concern, pointing out that "learning to read is critical to a child's overall well-being. If a youngster does not learn to read in our literacy-driven society, hope for a fulfilling, productive life diminishes" (Lyon, March 1998).

Noah Webster and Horace Mann found their challenges in the terrible physical condition of schools, the lack of any professional training for teachers, and the limited access to education for many children. Today those problems are largely resolved. Universal education and professional, respectful treatment of children in schools are the norm. In our time, reading failure is among the most pressing educational challenges. It will take time to change the direction of teacher training and to develop instructional programs suitable to the full range of reading aptitude, but in the meantime a number of communities are already taking positive steps. For example, some school districts have limited class size to fewer than twenty children in the early elementary grades, and made reading instruction the top priority. In-service training in reading instruction is proliferating, as school districts start to offer highly rated programs rather than forcing teachers to seek them out on their own. The federal government, following up on the NICHD research findings, has launched a number of new reading initiatives such as the Reading Excellence Act of 1998.

Given the advances of recent years, we have reason to be optimistic. Today there is increasing public concern about the need for educational reform in general, and attention to reading failure in particular. The federal government continues to invest in well-designed longitudinal research, which has already produced important findings that are reaching public awareness, albeit slowly. Teacher training programs may be ready for change, and in the meantime countless dedicated teachers search for ways to acquire research-based teaching methods and to tailor instruction to the needs of each child in their classrooms. Increasingly, parents concerned about their children's reading abilities are looking for information and help, appealing to teachers and principals, and organizing within communities in order to have a greater voice in obtaining appropriate services. There will always be some people with very severe dyslexia who will not be able to master the technical aspects of reading to a reasonable degree in spite of the most dedicated and appropriate teaching, but they are very few. Given early identification, intervention, and sufficient practice, today's student with dyslexia can be treated. Dyslexia is, indeed, both a treatable and a beatable condition. In general, we are headed in the right direction now. Growing awareness and persistent effort should keep us on course.

Social and institutional change take time. In the interim, parents and teachers can effect changes on a smaller scale that can be very helpful at home and at school. We will survey a wide range of practical measures in Chapter 8.

▶ 8

Prevention, Intervention, and Remediation

In this chapter we review a broad range of parenting, teaching, and tutoring activities designed to help in preventing, ameliorating, or overcoming reading difficulties. Although the main focus is on attending to the weaknesses associated with pure dyslexia, some of the ideas, materials, and programs apply to a wider array of reading problems and stem from general child development and educational principles as well as reading fundamentals.

The chapter is divided into three major sections. We begin with *primary prevention*, which means taking action against a potential problem before it occurs. Vaccinations and traffic lights are examples of primary prevention. The second section deals with *early intervention* (sometimes referred to as secondary prevention), which is used in instances of high risk or early symptoms, before significant problems have developed. Finally we will turn our attention to *remediation* (analogous to tertiary prevention in medical settings), which is necessary when significant problems are evident, and when earlier prevention and intervention efforts have been insufficient or lacking. The boundaries between these three types of prevention are not exact; once again we are dealing with a continuum rather than totally discrete categories.

PRIMARY PREVENTION

Primary prevention in the area of reading consists largely of providing children with a stimulating and enriching language environment at home, and good instructional programs at school. Most efforts at primary prevention focus on the preschool and early primary school years; the aim is to engender familiarity with, appreciation of, and a love for books, and to encourage the development of the perceptual, memory, and language skills that underlie learning to read.

Primary Prevention at Home

It is widely recognized that during the first years of childhood, parents play a large role in laying the groundwork for later school success. In recent years, with the emergence of family literacy programs, we often hear how important it is that parents read to their young children. But there are many other ways, some planned and some intuitive and spontaneous, in which parents are able to enrich the literacy-enhancing quality of their homelife. As role models, teachers, and loving caretakers, parents have the opportunity to saturate their children's early environment with the materials, activities, and adult encouragement that build both desire and competence for learning to read. The following are some of the ways they do this.

Infant and Toddler Years

Creating Interest and Pleasure in Books.   Children's books now come in all sizes, shapes, and materials. There are plastic books that can go in the bath, cloth books that can go in the bed, cardboard books that can tolerate a certain amount of licking, sucking, and chewing. There are very simple books with pictures of brightly colored objects, made up of eight pages or less. There are small, easy-to-grasp books with pages that can be turned by a child under 1 year.

The presence of books at this early age makes them familiar items, in the same way that rubber bath toys and stuffed animals become familiar and appealing objects. Books for very young children are designed to engage their developing interests and capabilities. Some have no text at all, only pictures of simple and brightly colored objects to look at and perhaps name. Some have highly repetitive text (The cow lives on the farm, The horse lives on the farm, The chicken lives on the farm, and so on) thereby creating pleasing rhythm and a high degree of predictability, attributes that small children enjoy. Repetitive, predictable text helps many children memorize books long before they can read, allowing them to enjoy their own participation in the activity and its accompanying sense of mastery.

Introducing the Names of Objects and Concepts into Daily Language. This is one aspect of a broader category sometimes referred to as *indirect teaching*. Parents are the earliest and probably the most powerful teachers of their children, and most of their teaching is carried out through daily life example and interaction, rather than through direct teaching. Direct teaching at this age is the sort used to teach a child to use the potty, or not to run in the street. Its role should be negligible or nonexistent in the primary prevention of reading difficulty, which in these years relies largely on exposure and does not require that the child master a skill or learn a lesson.

In the early childhood years, before formal school entry into kindergarten and first grade, the names of *colors*, *numbers*, and *alphabet* letters are major items in the "curriculum" of indirect teaching. Because they are not concrete objects, learning the words that name them is a more abstract and difficult task than learning the names of other things (such as parts of the body, household objects, toys, and animals). In kindergarten and in some preschools they are taught in a more formal and organized way, but for toddlers at home indirect teaching is more appropriate. Early, indirect exposure is helpful in two ways: Children entering preschool programs are more comfortable and confident when the language of this early curriculum echoes their familiar home experience; and the few children who have not learned what most toddlers know, in spite of exposure at home, can be identified for early intervention.

A special merit of indirect teaching is the absence of pressure on the child to learn, which spares him any sense of failing or disappointing the parent. Words and concepts to be learned are simply embedded in daily speech. Thus, a parent starting to teach her child the names of *colors*, rather than saying "Let's put on your shirt," will say "Let's put on your blue shirt." Adults pointing out interesting things around them can make it a habit to use color words whenever appropriate: "Do you see that red bird up in the tree?" If a father says to his daughter, "Bring me your green socks" and she brings the yellow ones, he does not tell her she made a mistake. Instead, he says, "Oh, you brought the yellow ones. Aren't they pretty? See how nice they look with your yellow sweater." Use of crayons and markers along with talking about the pictures and the colors provides repeated practice in learning color names.

This indirect teaching approach is the same method that the Whole Language Movement has been recommending for learning to identify words. We have seen in Chapter 7 why direct instruction is more appropriate for that basic reading skill, but in these first few years of life and learning, when the aim is *language* acquisition rather than reading acquisition, the whole language approach is exactly right. The emphasis is on meaning and pleasure, children are surrounded with materials to experience and enjoy, and they are expected to learn, through exposure and encouragement, when they are ready.

In regard to *numbers*, the first stage of learning about them is discovering what the number words mean. To teach the meaning of number words, parents can begin by introducing the words *one*, *two*, and *three* in natural situations. For example, "There's one cookie left on the plate," or "You may have two pieces of candy after dinner," later to be followed by counting them out: "one, two." At this point, it's not the counting that is important, but rather what the counting words mean. We want the *word one* to become attached to the *concept* of *one*, which is best grasped by seeing it repeatedly in different contexts. We can't point to *one* the way we can point to a table. *One* has to be illustrated repeatedly—one table, one doll, one sock, one cookie.

These are the years for learning the easiest, lowest number words. One and two are a good beginning, and working up to five allows parents to make use of children's fingers and toes for illustration. In fact, any examples involving the child's or the parent's features will be useful: two eyes, two ears, one nose, and so on. Being visible and touchable and having personal meaning all make them excellent learning aids.

With the focus of the infancy and toddler years on language development rather than reading, there is no reason for parents to introduce *alphabet* letters as items to be recognized. At this stage of development our main interest is in imparting the larger elements of language—words, phrases, and sentences—and their meanings. Children who show spontaneous interest in letters that they come across (in places like blocks, *Sesame Street*, or the refrigerator) should of course have their questions answered, and those who persist should be taken seriously. However, at this stage, rhyme is the most important smaller-than-a-word language element that children need to encounter and enjoy.

Rhyme.   Rhyme a long-standing and much loved staple of childhood has recently taken on new significance in the field of reading acquisition and in primary prevention of reading difficulties. As a consequence of extensive research on phonological and phonemic awareness as precursors to successful reading (Blachman, 1996; Lyon, 1996; Torgesen, 1997), much greater attention is now given to a child's ability to identify rhyming sounds. As discussed in Chapter 2, readers and spellers need to be able to distinguish the individual phoneme sounds that make up words; to return to the usual example, they have to be able to hear the 'c' and 'a' and 't' sounds in *cat*. It's a much easier task to distinguish rhyming sounds, which generally occur at the syllable level and are therefore more easily perceived. At the syllable level, it is sufficient to hear that the /ay/ in *play* and *stay* is the same sound and creates rhyme.

Our culture is richly endowed with nursery rhymes, poems written for children, rhyming stories like *The Cat in the Hat*, and children's songs and chants. These are easily incorporated into the mix of parent-child activities, not only when children are being read to but at other companionable times, including riding in the car. In these first years, children do not need to be talked to about rhyming. Hearing, reciting, singing, and enjoying rhymes are the experiences they need now. In a very few years, it will be part of the foundation they lean on when they are asked to be more consciously aware and analytic as words are divided up into sounds, and sounds are blended into words.

A number of resource books are now available to parents, teachers, and other caregivers of very young children, containing rhymes and songs, activities, and extensive listings of books. One of these, *Toddle on Over: Developing Infant & Toddler Literature Programs*, is listed in Appendix B.

Toddlerhood to Kindergarten
With wide variations in timing, children move out of toddlerhood sometime around age 3. We stop thinking of them as toddlers as they achieve greater fluency and coordination, not only in walking, but also in speaking, in small motor activities including drawing and handling toys and utensils, and in large motor activities such as climbing and tricycle riding. Their advancing skill levels along with their rapidly increasing vocabulary and knowledge allow them to take a more active and demonstrable role in their ongoing learning at home.

Libraries, Books, and Reading.   During these years, books continue to have great physical appeal with their colorful and entertaining pictures, attractive pullout segments, and items to manipulate. At the same time, along with the increase in attention span, general knowledge, and coordination, the children are also progressing in the particular cognitive skills that support reading acquisition—perception, memory, and language competence. As a result, they are able and eager to engage in more wide-ranging and complex activities connected with books and reading.

The children are increasingly able to handle longer and more complicated stories, and to participate in conversations about them. Interest in a specific subject area (such as frogs, snakes, princesses, rainbows, dinosaurs, ballerinas, trains, spaceships, baby animals) often develops during this period, and books about the subject, fiction or nonfiction, are then particularly welcome. This is an excellent time to become regular patrons of the public library, perhaps to find books on the favorite topics, but in any event to begin what we hope will become a lifelong and rewarding association.

Fostering a child's relationship with the *library* offers many benefits and is an important part of primary prevention. The range and nature of materials offered continue to expand, and already encompass music recordings, videos, films, and computer activities, along with a large variety of books for all ages and interests of childhood. Libraries also offer children special activities such as story reading hours, and in some instances have developed programs for children from infancy onward that include all the primary prevention activities noted in this chapter, and more.

In addition to the materials and activities that libraries offer, and for some just as important, is the friendly, welcoming, and helpful environment that most *librarians* create. Librarians, like parents and teachers, find their job satisfaction in helping children to be successful and happy. And librarians have several advantages over parents and teachers: they have extensive if not unlimited resources to offer in their particular bailiwick; they have a more objective, less emotionally freighted relationship with each child; and that relationship does not require the child to produce something that meets a set standard. Librarians are there to help, not to approve or disapprove. Small children establish comfortable associations and trusting relationships in the library during the years of looking at picture books, listening to stories being read, and selecting books to take home on their own card. Later, it will be easier to turn to librarians for help in locating suitable material for their school assignments and at the appropriate reading level, even if they are weak readers.

In addition to books from the library, *books at home* that a child can keep and have immediate access to are also important. In recognition of this fact, and to assist and encourage parents to provide literacy-enhancing activities at home, a number of pediatric literacy programs have been set up in doctors' offices and pediatric clinics around the country. One of the first of these, at Boston City Hospital, gave a picture book at each pediatric visit to every child between 6 months and 5 years of age. Needlman (1997) evaluated a number of these programs and found that giving books to the children led to an increase in reading activities at home. In a similar vein, there are a number of home-based programs that offer parents the opportunity to have a teacher come to their home. The teacher reads to the children, demonstrating techniques for engaging children as young as 2 in listening to stories and developing a love of books. Ryan (1999) describes one of these programs, the Parent-Child Home Program, which has been in existence for about thirty years and is offered in many American cities as well as in other countries (see Appendix B).

Increasing Attention to Words and Letters. During these years preceding more formal instruction, children at home engage in activities that mimic their parents' (and perhaps their older siblings') reading and writing. Children are natural imitators, and much of their learning comes from observing adults and then approximating what they have witnessed, to the best of their ability at the moment. They may hold an open book and pretend to be reading, or make random marks on a sheet of paper and tell you what it says. They are by nature highly motivated to move ahead, to do what the grown-ups do, and to show what they have accomplished. In this period when parents are doing mostly indirect teaching, they are effectively *modeling* repeatedly in their routine behavior the abilities they expect their children to grow into. They then allow the children to proceed at their own pace, relying on the child's built-in drive to become more and more accomplished. Magnetic refrigerator letters, and paper and markers for making lists and writing letters, are among the materials, along with books, that young children can play with and use as props in pretending to be competent readers and writers.

As they get a little older, some children want to be able to make real words by themselves, and to recognize certain written words. At that point parents take a more direct role in identifying certain letters by name, writing a word for a child to copy, perhaps demonstrating how some letters are made. Many children enjoy learning to write and recognize their own name, family members' names, and other words that have special significance to them. When the child is engaged in and enjoying the activity, this shift from indirect to direct teaching is successful so long as it follows the child's interests and curiosity, rather than the parent's drive to impart knowledge. It is important not to push formal instruction on young children in the belief that certain things must be mastered by a certain time. In *Preventing Reading Difficulties in Young Children*, Snow, Burns, and Griffin (1998) review a number of studies of family literacy activities in the years preceding kindergarten, and note that "Children who learn from their parents that literacy is a source of enjoyment may be more motivated to persist in their efforts to learn to read despite difficulties they may encounter during the early (school) years" (p. 143).

Singing songs and reciting nursery rhymes and other familiar poems and stories, in unison or individually, help increase vocabulary and develop sensitivity to rhyme. During the nursery school and kindergarten years these are likely to include the alphabet song and various counting songs and chants (for example, "one potato, two potato, three potato, four") that help establish these sequences in a rote form. For the alphabet in particular, being able to sing the entire alphabet from memory equips the child with a built-in reference tool, in case he has difficulty later on when he has to identify the letters in print.

> *Jimmy, age 6, was in first grade and struggling with reading. Showing him the alphabet printed out in capital letters, I pointed to the 'G' and asked, "What letter is this?" He thought for a few moments, and then began singing the alphabet song, pointing to each letter in turn as he sang. As his finger reached the letter 'G' he heard himself singing 'G.' With a smile of accomplishment he looked up from the page and said, "That's 'G.' "*

Finally, there are many games and activities that increase exposure to and familiarity with letters, words, and numbers. Card games such as Fish and Old Maid, and dominoes, are among the traditional games that familiarize children with numbers and the numerals that represent them. Simple board games such as Candyland give children practice in counting spaces with a finger, coordinating their visual-motor activity on the board with their counting aloud. Activity books offer games and puzzles that require perceiving, matching, and remembering letters.

The School Years

Primary prevention continues beyond the early years of learning to read, into learning to enjoy reading. Some children enjoy reading on their own as much as they enjoyed being read to, but many become engaged in a broad variety of activities and turn away from independent reading. With the variety of distractions and competition for children's attention, many students read only what they must for school, and look elsewhere for pleasure and relaxation. Using leisure time for activities such as sports, paid or volunteer work, movies, and spending time with friends becomes increasingly attractive as children move beyond the early primary grades.

Parents who enjoy reading and place high value on its contributions both to personal pleasure and to academic and professional achievement are often distressed by the failure of their young and adolescent offspring to read for pleasure. Some of these parents want not only that their children read for enjoyment, but that they read works of literary value. For example, one father whose daughter was reading romantic fiction kept after her to read "the classics" instead. In general, it is a mistake to push children to read material that doesn't interest them as a leisure-time activity. Although it is important that parents support children in meeting their school obligations, dictating the nature of their free time is likely to backfire, because parental pressure often stiffens resistance. As to the classics, it is never too late to discover and appreciate them when they are encountered through school assignments, recommendations from friends, or films.

Mary Leonhardt is a high school English teacher who wrote *Parents Who Love Reading, Kids Who Don't* (1993), a book filled with suggestions for helping children find or rediscover the pleasures of reading. She stresses the importance of keeping reading an enjoyable activity, with material that the children can easily connect to. This includes magazines about current interests (such as sports), joke books, baseball cards, comic books, and the sports pages of the newspaper. Leonhardt encourages parents to continue reading aloud after the children have learned to read on their own, and to take turns reading. Parents can enliven the reading by such maneuvers as "hamming it up" and by making mistakes that children can correct.

A study surveying 419 sixth graders, "What Johnny Likes to Read Is Hard to Find in School" (Worthy, Moorman, & Turner, 1999), found that the materials most preferred were scary stories and books, and cartoons and comics, cited by 66 percent and 65 percent of the children, respectively. Next were popular magazines (38 percent), sports books (33 percent), and drawing books (29 percent). Another 20 to 22 percent of the children cited books on cars and trucks, animal stories, series books, and funny novels.

Series books such as *Goosebumps, Hardy Boys, American Girls Collection, Nancy Drew,* and *Baby-Sitters Club* are very helpful because they provide a long supply of reading material and because many children, once they've "met" the main characters, are highly motivated to read more of the series—the attraction is analogous to the appeal of one's favorite TV sitcom. The literary quality may not be high, but at this point that is not important. For otherwise reluctant readers, the experience of reading for pleasure is a sufficiently worthy achievement.

Primary Prevention at School

Having concentrated throughout this book on reading instruction from first grade on, we are going to focus here on kindergarten programming in the service of primary prevention. Kindergarten is a critical place in the transition from disparate experiences at home, day care, and nursery school to the nearly universal expectation of first grade: that children will begin learning to read in a structured setting with built-in expectations about what is to be learned and at what rate. Snow and her colleagues (1998) highlight two paramount goals of kindergarten: The first is "to ensure that children leave kindergarten familiar with the structural elements and organization of print." The second is "to establish perspectives and attitudes on which learning about and from print depend; it includes motivating children to be literate and making them feel like successful learners" (p. 179). We look first at some familiar materials and activities that promote these goals, and then at phonemic awareness, an important concept that is relatively new and not widely recognized among those outside the reading research community.

Traditional Kindergarten Activities
Reading aloud allows children to enjoy many aspects of books, including story content, pictures, interaction with other children as well as the teacher, and sharing personal experiences

related to the book. When reading aloud is done with familiar, repeatedly read, oversize storybooks, and the teacher points to words and phrases of familiar text or rhyme, children pick up knowledge about print conventions such as left-to-right directionality, and words as single entities separated by spaces. At the same time they are taking in the language and concepts embedded in the material, and developing their capacities to express ideas in a coherent form. This is especially important for children who have had little or no story reading experience before kindergarten.

Language experience charts and related activities that put children's words into print demonstrate the connections between spoken and written language. Seeing their own words put into print is intrinsically satisfying, and it also stimulates their interest in being able to do the writing themselves. *Writing and recognition of letters and a few words* introduces children to the tasks that will become more intensive and formalized in first grade.

Phonemic Awareness

Because research has consistently demonstrated that phonemic awareness is a critical skill underlying reading ability, there is increasing interest in including it in the school curriculum, especially in kindergarten and first grade. Torgesen (1999) defines phonemic awareness as the ability to understand "that a single-syllable word such as *cat*, which is experienced by the listener as a single beat of sound, actually can be subdivided into beginning, middle, and ending sounds. It also involves the idea, or understanding, that individual segments of sound at the phonemic level can be combined together to form words" (p. 129). Torgesen, who has studied and conducted research on phonemic awareness for many years, notes that children become increasingly skilled over time at noticing and manipulating the phoneme sounds of words. Their development can be observed as they advance from kindergarten through elementary school grades. Between first and second grade a child can be expected to advance from being able to isolate and pronounce only the initial sound in a word like *cat*, to being able to segment all the sounds in words that have three and four phonemes.

Children have an easier time developing awareness of individual phonemes when they have had prior and repeated experience in noticing larger elements of sound. These larger elements include rhymes, sounds in the environment such as the ticking of clocks and the singing of birds, and utterances that are not quite words such as "sh" (let's be quiet) and "brrr" (it's cold). Nursery school and kindergarten programs can highlight and reinforce these experiences, and move on to training the children to be aware of relatively large segments of words. With assorted games and activities, teachers draw the children's attention to compound words such as *snowplow* or *cowboy* ("What two words can you hear in this word?") and to the number of syllables that can be counted in words of varying lengths.

Training in phonemic awareness begins by paying attention only to the sounds in words, without reference to the letters and words in print, and early lessons usually start out with a focus on the initial phoneme. Here is an example of a teacher demonstrating the initial sound of a word by stressing and repeating it, from a curriculum guide, *Phonemic Awareness in Young Children* (Adams et al., 1997):

> *The teacher says "Guess whose name I am going to say now." She then says /d/ /d/ /d/ /d/ until a child calls out his own name or the name of a classmate, for example "Danny!" If there is also a David and a Diana in the group, those names will also be identified and the children will learn that the same phoneme can appear in many different words.*

At a later stage in the development of phonemic awareness, after children have learned to read some simple words, they will practice segmenting the *written* word into its component sounds. In addition to reinforcing their awareness of separate sounds, this part of the learning process repeatedly demonstrates that the sounds in words are represented in print by letters.

EARLY INTERVENTION

Early intervention plays a critically important role in the treatment of dyslexia. There is strong and ever-increasing evidence that early attention to word identification problems is effective for many children in *preventing* the development of reading problems that persist through the grades (Foorman, Francis, & Fletcher, 1997; Francis et al., 1996; Torgesen, 1997). Three types of early intervention are presented in this section. The first proceeds case by case, beginning with identification by a parent or teacher of a child experiencing difficulty, followed by assessment and appropriate remedial intervention. The second, developed in recent years, is the deployment of a controlled, prepackaged program in entire classrooms, and in some cases entire schools, in which children are judged to be at risk for school failure in general and for reading difficulties in particular. The third type combines important elements of the first two.

Early Intervention with Individuals

In most cases, identification of a child's reading difficulties is made at school, but it is not uncommon for parents to be first to sound the alarm. Some children struggle hard to keep up, and do not complain or ask for help at school; but at home they talk about not being able to do their work as well, or as fast, as the other children. Some children do not directly say they are worried about not being able to read well, but they express their sadness or anxiety in other ways: sleep or appetite problems, reluctance to go to school, irritability, tearfulness, and other behavior. No matter who first identifies the problem, good home-school communication and cooperation are essential ingredients in getting a remedial program under way.

One basic technique for helping children with weak reading skills is a standard remedial education practice often referred to as *diagnostic-prescriptive teaching*. The terminology is medical, but the process is more like what goes on in a health club or music lesson. The knowledgeable classroom teacher or reading specialist does an assessment to determine which skills are weak or lacking, and then plans a series of lessons to promote the development of deficient skills while making use of apparent strengths.

A Sample (Partial) Teaching Plan

To illustrate diagnostic-prescriptive teaching, let's take the reading weaknesses of Sally, whose case was presented in Chapter 6, and imagine her reading tutor's response:

- Sally worked very slowly.
- She misread a number of easy words, but got them right the second time.
- She was weak on digraphs.
- She was weak on vowel sounds.

Sally's tutor, Amalia, can be expected to think along the following lines:

- Sally's reading speed is slow, but attempts to increase it should wait until she has better mastery of the code and can read with more consistent accuracy.
- Her misreading of simple words (which she can read correctly when asked to look again) is another indication that she needs extra time for accurate word recognition.
- She seems to know how to pronounce digraphs (/ch/, /th/, and so on), but she does not automatically recognize them when she comes upon them in print and has a tendency to pronounce them as single consonants (/c/, /t/, and so on).
- Her familiarity with short vowel sounds is unsteady. Regarding both digraphs and vowels, Sally has some knowledge about these elements of the code (*cognizance*), but has

not *mastered* them and is far from *automaticity* in her response to them.

Amalia will also make some tentative assumptions about the severity of Sally's reading difficulty. She will consider two major factors: (1) how far behind Sally is in her skill acquisition, relative to the average student midway through the second-grade year; and (2) how quickly she will be able to learn the necessary elements to the level of mastery or automaticity required to close the gap. In judging how far behind Sally is, Amalia will be helped by formal test scores, informal surveys of skills, and observations of Sally's speed and accuracy in processing written language. At least as important, however, is Amalia's knowledge about the sequence of skill development involved in learning to read, and her appraisal of how far Sally has progressed on the path to reading. Sally is weak in being able to quickly and accurately apply her knowledge about digraphs and vowel sounds, but she has begun to learn them. Otherwise, her decoding skills are good, and she has a good sight vocabulary. In regard to the second factor—how quickly Sally will learn—Amalia can be optimistic in light of all that Sally has learned so far, coupled with her persistence and good intelligence.

Many tutors plan their sessions (usually thirty to sixty minutes) to follow a routine sequence of activities, usually including some skills practice, some reading of text, and some games that reinforce the skills being learned and review those previously taught. Amalia will decide whether they should begin by working on both digraphs and vowels in the early lessons. Because Sally is a highly motivated and persistent second grader, Amalia will probably decide to plan lessons and activities in both. If she has misjudged Sally's patience, endurance, and learning speed, she will limit the amount of challenging, frustrating material that Sally encounters, and use more of their time together to strengthen Sally's command of more familiar elements.

The essence of remedial work is *breaking down the task* into smaller elements that can be practiced and then integrated back into the larger unit. Amalia will start work with Sally on digraphs by showing her words that contain them. If Sally isn't able to remember the sounds for several digraphs (for example, /ch/, /ph/, /th/) Amalia will break down the task further and concentrate on one of them, let's say /ch/.

Once the target element to be learned has been determined, *practice* ensues, in as many forms and sensory modalities as are necessary to establish the symbol-sound connection in Sally's mind. They will look together at 'ch' words that Sally already knows as sight words: *child, chicken, chapter, teacher, lunch,* and so on. They will build words with anagram letters: *chip, chin, chat, chop, chest, choo-choo train.* Sally will read lists of 'ch' words, and then mixed word lists, with 'ch' words and 'c' words and other words. Amalia will pronounce 'ch' words for Sally to spell aloud, and also to write. If Sally, her parents, and Amalia think it's a good idea, some of the practice drills and games may be done at home too. When Sally reads regular text during her lessons, Amalia will be noting how well she does with 'ch' words when they are embedded in the running material. When Sally shows mastery of 'ch,' she and Amalia will start working on the other digraphs, while continuing to review those she has already learned. Either simultaneously or later, Sally and Amalia will do similar exercises and practice sessions with the vowel sounds.

Sally (whom we know from the assessment to have a mild problem) made good progress, but a child with more severe dyslexia is likely to take a longer time to learn the elements of the code and also to have difficulty retaining what she learned. In that case, Amalia would have to consider recommending a more intensive program for her, in which more time and resources would be devoted to teaching her to read.

In our hypothetical lessons we gave Sally one-to-one tutoring. The same kind of teaching can also be successful with small groups of children, usually two to five in number. Although one-to-one tutoring can be tailored specifically to the strengths and weaknesses of the student, there are advantages to small-group tutoring and in some instances it is preferable. Some children enjoy the group camaraderie, some need a break from the steady attention of the tutor, some are strengthened by seeing that others have similar or greater difficulties and that they can help another child. In many schools, children with reading difficulties have both individual and small-group lessons each week.

Lack of Identification: The Major Impediment to Early Intervention

The challenge of early intervention lies not in what or how to teach the approximately 20 percent of children who will have difficulty in learning to read. The requisite teaching materials and methods are well developed, and have been used for many years with good results. Children identified with dyslexia ranging from mild to very severe have been successfully treated by trained tutors and teachers for many years. The challenge lies in educating schoolteachers and administrators in methods of early identification and intervention that are presently available but not at all widespread.

Lack of School Resources. From my experience and observations in the past thirty-five years, most treated dyslexic students have been assessed and taught by private practitioners and at special schools for learning disabled children. I have known a few private schools and public school systems that move proactively to identify children with reading difficulties in the early grades, and provide them with in-school remedial teaching that includes direct phonics instruction. These are usually well-endowed schools and communities that can offer smaller classes, more experienced classroom teachers, and well-trained reading specialists. They are the exception and not the rule. Curtis and Longo (1999) note that teachers rarely get formal training in how to teach "hard-to-teach" kids, and a *New York Times* editorial (1997) reported that according to National Institutes of Health researchers, "fewer than ten percent of teachers actually know how to teach reading to children who don't get it automatically."

Outmoded Federal Regulations.   In 1975 Congress passed
Public Law 94-142, the first comprehensive legislation guaranteeing the right of all children with disabilities to an appropriate, publicly supported education. In 1977, in specifying
what constitutes various disabilities, the Federal Register de-
fined *learning disability* as:

> *a severe discrepancy between achievement and intellec-*
> *tual ability in one or more of the areas: (1) oral expres-*
> *sion; (2) listening comprehension; (3) written expression;*
> *(4) basic reading skill; (5) reading comprehension; (6)*
> *mathematics calculation; or (7) mathematics reasoning.*
> *The child may not be identified as having a specific*
> *learning disability if the discrepancy between ability*
> *and achievement is primarily the result of: (1) a visual,*
> *hearing, or motor handicap; (2) mental retardation; (3)*
> *emotional disturbance; or (4) environmental, cultural,*
> *or economic disadvantage (cited in Fletcher, 1998).*

Requiring a *severe discrepancy* between intelligence and
achievement as a qualifying characteristic of specific learning
disability was consistent with the popular understanding of
learning disabilities in the 1970s. At that time, there was still
a widespread belief that learning disabilities were limited to
those with average and above-average intelligence, and that
the disability represented a striking difference in overall functioning. As discussed in Chapter 3, that is one of the continuing myths about learning disabilities. Since that time a strong
consensus has developed among researchers that learning
disabilities are not confined to those with average or above-
average intelligence, and that the *IQ discrepancy model*, in and
of itself, is not useful for identifying children with reading disabilities (Fletcher, 1998; Siegel, 1989; Stanovich & Siegel,
1994). Although an uneven profile of cognitive abilities remains
a major characteristic of those with learning disabilities, overall level of intelligence and IQ scores are inappropriate gauges
of that profile. Unfortunately, federal regulations have not kept

up with research findings, although an unsuccessful effort was made to change these regulations when the comprehensive legislation (now called Individuals with Disabilities Education Act, or IDEA) was renewed in 1997.

As the IQ discrepancy model continues to determine perspective and policy in school settings, it has a highly deleterious effect on the early identification of children with dyslexia. Children referred for assessment of reading difficulty in the early grades are frequently disqualified for a diagnosis of learning disability because they don't meet the IQ discrepancy requirement of the federal definition. And in many states and local school districts, a child with reading problems who doesn't officially qualify as learning disabled not only will go undiagnosed as dyslexic, but will also fail to receive any additional services in reading instruction.

When the classroom teacher refers Jane for assessment of her reading problem, it is generally because she has neither the time nor the expertise herself to help Jane. If Jane is not recognized as reading disabled because the IQ discrepancy is not great enough, her teacher may or may not receive advice on how to assist Jane in the regular classroom. There are also many first- and second-grade teachers who will not make the referral in the first place, because they believe or hope that she will outgrow her difficulties, or because they have no confidence that a referral will result in assistance for either Jane or her teacher. Fletcher (1998) has noted that a number of recent intervention studies "have generated remarkably good results in enhancing the word recognition skills of children at risk for reading problems because of poor literacy experiences, poor phonological processing skills, and/or poor word recognition skills, and represent *prevention* studies based on early identification. However, the intervention models in these studies could not be implemented because of the reliance on IQ discrepancy as the basis for description of a learning disability. Hence, *discrepancy prevents prevention*" (p. 11).

The importance of early identification and intervention cannot be overstated. Children who have trouble reading tend to avoid it, and therefore do not get the practice required to read more easily. They fall further and further behind, not only in reading skills but frequently in vocabulary, general knowledge, verbal fluency, and written expression. They do not catch up without intensive help, and the longer that help is delayed the greater the gap that has to be closed. In the meantime, as failures pile up and adolescence approaches, the likelihood of school dropout, with its attendant social and economic consequences, is heightened. This scenario is played out repeatedly, especially among the disadvantaged in large urban areas. Since the 1960s, a number of large-scale projects have been launched in hopes of altering this all-too-familiar pattern of failure.

Early Intervention with Targeted Populations

In the idealistic, activist atmosphere of President Lyndon Johnson's War on Poverty, the 1960s witnessed the beginning of large-scale federal programs designed to serve disadvantaged children at high risk for school failure. *Head Start*, providing teacher training, classes for preschoolers, and outreach to their families, has been widely regarded as successful and continues to the present. *Title I* of the Elementary and Secondary Education Act of 1965 was designed to help disadvantaged children by offering more money to state and local school districts, but it did not provide a specific program or policy for assisting children at risk (Snow, Burns, & Griffin, 1998). Renamed *Chapter I* in the 1981 reauthorization of the program, some programmatic requirements were included but they did not extend to the specifics of teaching reading. In general, the results of Chapter I programs have been disappointing. In some evaluative studies, children receiving services were found to have made some improvement, but not to the extent that brought them up to the level of their classmates (Carter, 1984; Puma et al., 1997).

Follow Through was seen as a "sequel" to Head Start. When it became apparent that the educational gains made by disadvantaged children in Head Start programs were not sustained over their elementary school years, the government launched Follow Through, to continue services to those children from kindergarten through third grade. Follow Through was an extremely ambitious program, designed to determine which of twenty contrasting educational models would be most successful in building and maintaining the educational progress of disadvantaged children. The programs differed in philosophical and pedagogical approaches; some concentrated on basic academic skills, some on conceptual development, and some on personality factors including self-esteem, curiosity, and persistence (Snow, Burns, & Griffin, 1998).

In many ways the evaluation results of Follow Through were disappointing. There were greater discrepancies in results within models than between models. However, one clear positive finding was that the direct instruction model, which taught basic skills in reading, arithmetic, and language, was effective for children who spent all four years in the program, and that the gains they made held up over time as indicated by test scores in later grades (Gersten, 1984). In spite of this positive finding about the effects of direct instruction, the lessons of Follow Through were not integrated into general education methodology, and direct instruction fell out of favor in many quarters with the spread of the Whole Language Movement.

The government programs of the 1960s and 1970s were launched in the spirit of President Johnson's "Great Society" and the War on Poverty. They had ambitious goals but did not monitor the nature of the curriculum or the quality of services at the classroom level. Since then, we have seen growing numbers of disadvantaged children, especially in large urban areas, an increasing shortage of adequately trained teachers of reading, and a society that relies more and more on an educated workforce. In part as a result of these societal changes, and in keeping with a major shift in political and economic trends over the same period, the 1980s and 1990s have seen the development of a different type of early intervention in schools, not by the government but by private organizations.

In the 1980s many states began measuring the performance of their public schools by requiring standardized testing in reading and math, and when individual schools or entire school districts consistently did poorly, their schools have frequently been taken over by outside authorities. In many instances, the new authority has adopted what are known as "whole school" designs, ready-made programs covering the broad areas of curriculum, teaching techniques, school organization, parent-school relations, and social service linkages. One of these programs focuses intensively on reading: Success for All, reported by Lemann (1998) as the largest and most popular of whole school designs, was operating in more than eleven hundred schools in the United States as of November 1998.

Success for All was created by Robert Slavin, an education researcher at the Center for Research on Effective Schooling for Disadvantaged Students, at Johns Hopkins University. Slavin recognized that traditional elementary school practice works against the principles of prevention and early intervention, providing kindergarten and first-grade teaching that is adequate for most students, and then assuming that "since most students do succeed with standard instruction in the early grades, there must be something wrong with those who do not." He describes the program this way:

> *The idea behind Success for All is to use everything known about effective instruction for students at risk to direct all aspects of school and classroom organization toward the goal of preventing academic deficits from appearing in the first place, recognizing and intensively intervening with any deficits that do appear, and providing students with a rich and full curriculum to enable them to build on their firm foundation in basic skills. The commitment of Success for All is to do whatever it takes to see that every child makes it through third grade at or near grade level in reading and other basic skills, and then goes beyond this in the later grades (Slavin et al., 1994, p. 176).*

Success for All began in one Baltimore public school in 1986, and has since spread around the country, operating mainly in large urban systems including Miami and New York City. (At a cost of $70,000 per school in the first year and $25,000 a year thereafter, it is used almost exclusively in poor schools; they can best afford it because federal Chapter I funds cover the direct costs.) It has programs available for preschool through third-grade classrooms. It provides daily lesson plans and materials, along with teacher training to the local school staff so they will deliver the program exactly as it was designed. First graders with reading problems receive individual tutoring. Children are assessed every eight weeks, and then regrouped every time for small-group instruction according to their skill level. A family support team works to make families feel comfortable in the school, to support student learning in the home, and to arrange for social and medical services when needed.

Evaluation studies have been carried out routinely, with children in the program compared to control groups. Reading scores for children in the program were consistently higher, and follow-up research indicates that gains achieved were maintained after the children finished the program. The program is generally regarded as successful, although it has worked better at its original sites where the program designers have been most closely involved (Snow, Burns, & Griffin, 1998). We have to be pleased about a method that puts the essential tool of reading into the hands of many children who would otherwise be well on their way to school failure by fourth grade. At the same time, the mechanistic qualities of the program, with its timetables and frequent shifting of groupings and teachers (Lemann [1998] draws analogies to marine boot camps and factory assembly lines), raises concerns about the effects of the process.

One concern about Success for All and similar whole school programs is the accompanying loss of autonomy in schools, from the principal's office to the teacher's classroom. When an outside organization like Success for All develops the curriculum, chooses the materials, tightly controls and scripts the daily lesson plans, and sends site visitors to monitor compliance, the role of the classroom teacher is dramatically altered. Teachers have to function more as technicians operating according to a manual of instructions, and less as self-directed professionals using their experience, knowledge, and creative talents to educate children.

To a degree, the teachers have consented to this change in role, because Success for All will not contract with a school until at least 80 percent of the teachers vote by secret ballot in favor of the program (Lemann, 1998). Although the teachers have given formal consent, one wonders what effect the changed atmosphere and the diminution of direct responsibility and professional autonomy have on their professional identity, their morale, and their relationships as nurturing caretakers to their young pupils. The third example of early intervention presents a model more likely to offer both the professional and personal qualities desired in reading education for all children.

Early Proactive Intervention with Small Groups

This type of intervention is in place in a number of independent schools and public school systems. It falls somewhere between the individual, case-by-case approach in which identification is made by a parent or teacher when a child shows signs of failure, and the whole class or whole school approach, which proceeds proactively on the assumption that many will fail unless strong preventive measures are taken. It is a natural consequence of the realization by school administrators that there will always be some children who find learning to read a difficult chore; and that these children need a well-planned, structured program that operates for them alongside, or in place of, the regular reading curriculum. It requires that the principal and faculty develop a program for identifying those children and offering them small-group instruction, in addition to or in place of their regular classroom reading lessons.

Identification

Starting with identification, there are a number of ways in which schools can be proactive in early intervention. They can screen all prospective entering students, before school opens in September, and provide early intensive help for those who show signs of being at risk for reading difficulties. That is how Tim, discussed in Chapter 6, was discovered to be a candidate for early assistance and eventual success as a reader and as a student. Nicholas, also presented in Chapter 6, was less fortunate because no one at his school was looking for, or able to recognize, the signs of dyslexia.

Another form of proactive early intervention is the surveying of all students in the early grades at specific points in the school year. This can be done by having classroom teachers refer any weak students to a reading specialist for assessment, or by administering an assessment measure to every student. Individual rather than group testing is very important for early intervention because it allows the examiner to observe how efficient (quick and accurate) the reading is. Thanks to the reading research studies sponsored by the federal government, for which a wide variety of assessment measures were developed, we are beginning to see the emergence of commercially available instruments that can test individual children quickly and efficiently. For example, the *Test of Word Reading Efficiency* (Torgesen, Wagner, & Rashotte, 1999) takes five to ten minutes per child, is suitable for all schoolchildren ages 6 and older, and taps directly into word identification competence by having the child read as many sight words and pronounceable nonsense words as she can in a limited period of time.

A simple screening device like this can be used at all ages. It would identify students like Eileen in Chapter 6 and Tony in Chapter 3, whose reading difficulties went unnoticed until eighth grade. Eileen's very slow reading would be detected because she would be able to read so few sight words in the allotted time period compared to others her age. Tony's frequent decoding errors would be picked up as he tried to read at normal speed.

Intervention

Once children have been identified as needing extra reading help, they are grouped for extra instruction according to their skill levels and the nature of their difficulties. Small groups allow for many types of remedial activity; these include continuing practice in phonemic awareness, introducing and practicing code elements and sight words, reinforcing previously learned elements that have not yet been adequately mastered, and previewing and reviewing lessons currently being presented in the larger classroom. In addition, the group can read together books or teacher-prepared stories in which vocabulary is sufficiently controlled to allow the children to correctly read most of the words.

In the small group, the teacher is able not only to know what each child has difficulty with, but also to plan tasks that allow each child to be successful much of the time. For example, during a short lesson on phonics, the teacher asks each child in turn to read a flash card, and presents each one with words appropriate to his current skill level. A child who has been learning the short vowel sounds of 'a' and 'i' will get simple c-v-c (consonant-vowel-consonant) words, such as *map*, *kit*, *fan*, *tin*. Another child who is practicing consonant blends will get *clap*, *trim*, *clock*. For children whose reading problems are not related to pure dyslexia and its attendant difficulties in mastering the code, small-group instruction would focus more directly on vocabulary building and other aspects of reading comprehension.

When a teacher can work regularly with a small group, she has the opportunity to track closely each child's skill and confidence levels, and to arrange individual sessions from time to time as necessary. In some cases, she can instruct parents in how they can be helpful at home with particular books, games, flash card practice, and the like. Ideally, her role as helper and troubleshooter would include being available to the whole school community and not limited to the "official" special education enrollment. In that way, she could consult with parents of children who, like Robert in Chapter 6, have weaknesses that lead them to shun reading at home but are not perceived at school as needing help.

REMEDIATION

When preventive measures and early intervention are not sufficient to teach children with dyslexia to read, they are given more specialized instruction carried out in small groups and individual tutoring. There are many programs and systems of specialized instruction, most of which are derived from a common set of principles. These principles were first formulated and developed into an instructional system by Anna Gillingham, a psychologist and a colleague of Samuel Orton; this system is now widely referred to as the *Orton-Gillingham method.* Gillingham, and her colleague Bessie Stillman, a remedial reading teacher, began using the method and training others to use it in the 1930s. The first bound edition of their teaching manual appeared in 1936, and they continued to revise it through the fifth edition in 1957 (Henry, 1998). It is currently available through Educators Publishing Service (Gillingham & Stillman, 1960).

The Orton-Gillingham Method

The Orton-Gillingham method relies heavily on *multisensory techniques*, which date back to the 1920s. When a teacher named Grace Fernald, in collaboration with Helen Keller, wrote about how she instructed her reading-impaired students to trace letters or words while saying the names aloud (Fernald & Keller, 1921; cited in Clark & Uhry, 1995). This procedure is known as the *VAKT approach* (visual, auditory, kinesthetic, tactile), in which sight, sound, movement, and touch are all activated in order to create as strong and lasting a memory as possible. Tracing is sometimes done in material such as sand where there are strong tactile and visual impressions as well as the kinesthetic sensation of movement. Tracing is sometimes carried out in the air, easier for children to do at their desks. No strong scientific evidence confirms the utility of multisensory instruction, but there is also little doubt that it has been effective. There are a number of speculative ideas about why it works: it keeps the student actively engaged on the task for longer periods of time than other methods, it cuts down boredom through varied methods of practice, the motor activity involved is a refreshing release, it provides more immediate and useful feedback to both teacher and student (Clark & Uhry, 1995). In addition, some laboratory studies, such as Hulme's (1981) experiments, have shown the positive effects of tracing in heightening the ability of weak readers to remember letters and words.

The Orton-Gillingham method (or O-G) has become the basic model for other multisensory remedial programs for dyslexic students. The programs vary in some ways, mostly in the sequence in which new elements are to be learned and in the techniques that have been elaborated for engaging the multiple senses, and some of them are adapted for groups of children as well as individual students. But they have basic principles in common: direct instruction of phonics, multisensory instruction, and a structured program moving from simple to complex elements. The umbrella term most recently applied to this form of instruction is *Multisensory Structured Language Education (MSLE)*, but one continues to hear programs described as O-G based or O-G derived.

Orton-Gillingham Plus

As new MSLE programs were developed, often by educators who were trained in the original O-G method, new techniques and activities were added to the original sensory activities of looking, listening, feeling, and movement. Among the significant elements that have been added to the mix of multisensory experiences are: (1) a focus on the oral-motor activity involved in the production of speech sounds, and (2) the use of amusing stories and pictures to aid learning of letter names and letter sounds.

Oral-Motor Consciousness

Auditory Discrimination in Depth (A.D.D.) is a program developed by Charles and Patricia Lindamood (1975). In 1999 it was renamed the *Lindamood Phoneme Sequencing Program (LiPS)*. It was among the first programs to highlight the importance of phonemic awareness. Another innovation of the Lindamood program, now incorporated into many other programs, is the emphasis placed on students' conscious awareness of how they produce speech sounds. For example, the phonemes /b/ and /p/ are called *lip poppers*, /t/ and /d/ are *tip tappers*, and pictures are used to illustrate the position of the lips, teeth, and tongue when sounds are produced.

Entertaining Stories and Pictures as Mnemonic Aids

It is more difficult to learn to associate abstract symbols with each other (a grapheme with its letter name, or a grapheme with its phoneme) than to associate them with something more meaningful, concrete, or familiar. Therefore, a number of programs have incorporated storytelling and picture cues, which give the child something more memorable to hang onto, and serve as temporary conduits between the abstract symbols. Here is an example from *Reading by the Rules*, a program that uses this technique extensively. (See Figure 8-1)

In teaching a child the name of the letter *Y*, the child is shown a card with this picture on it and told the following story:

> *Mom sent you to get ready for bed. When she came to say goodnight, she found you like this. She said, "Why are you on your head?" What does Mom ask?*

In subsequent practice sessions the child will be shown the card and asked to name the letter. If she cannot name the letter, she can be cued with the question, "What did his mom ask?" If the cue is not sufficient in helping the child recall the story and letter name, the story is told again. Eventually neither story nor cue will be necessary to make the association between the graphic symbol and the name of the letter.

FIGURE 8-1

Credit: Mnemonic Alphabet Wisnia-Kapp Reading
Programs; Peggy Radcliff, Designer.

Fluency

As they acquire a reasonable degree of mastery of the code,
some dyslexic children move naturally into reading text at the
Stage III level, integrating whole word recognition with analytic skills. They may start out slowly, building up speed and
accuracy as they go along, but they can achieve a comfortable
and steady reading pace without requiring extra effort beyond
regular reading practice. However, there are also many stu-

dents like Eileen (in Chapter 6), who have great difficulty reading connected text fluently without active and time-consuming decoding. They are having difficulty reaching Stage III, the mature and integrated reading stage, probably in part because they lack good Stage I abilities for global, holistic word recognition. Now, although they are familiar with the code, their weaknesses in whole word recognition interfere with the integration of "the whole and its parts" that is required for smooth, comfortably paced reading. Eileen's problem was not recognized until eighth grade, but students with this kind of difficulty can often be spotted by third grade, and sometimes earlier.

A number of techniques have been developed to promote fluency, and we will look at a few of them here.

Repeated Readings

Samuels's method of repeated reading is described in an article in *The Reading Teacher* (Samuels, 1979). In one of his studies, each student chose an easy, interesting story. Then a short passage of 50 to 200 words was marked off for practice. "The student read the short selection to an assistant, who recorded the reading speed and number of word recognition errors on a graph. . . . The student then returned to his/her seat and practiced reading the selection while the next student read to the assistant. When the first student's turn came again, the procedure was repeated until an 85 word per minute criterion rate was reached. Then the student went on to the next passage" (p. 404). Graphing the results, so that the student could see the reading rate go up and the number of errors go down, was a significant motivating feature. Samuels noted that some teachers considering repeated reading were concerned about boredom, but that, to the contrary, the students were excited by the gains they made in fluency.

Dowhower (1989) reports on a variety of ways to incorporate repeated reading into the regular classroom reading program. In one scenario, the teacher reads a story aloud to the group, then has them read it in unison with her, and finally each child practices a segment independently until criteria for accuracy and speed are reached. In another method, special areas are set up in the classroom or library where children can go to practice reading. They might be assisted by a teacher, another student, or taped stories as described next.

Listening and Reading

Chomsky (1978) developed a variation of repeated reading for five children reading at the bottom of their third-grade class; they lacked fluency, hated reading, and avoided it whenever possible. She provided tape-recorded stories for the children to listen to as they followed along in the accompanying book. The children listened while following the print until they were able to read a book on their own, working largely independently and practicing segments of text until they had achieved mastery over a whole book (usually 20 to 30 pages). In large measure they had memorized the books from repeated listenings, but they had also learned to recognize more words on sight, evidenced by significantly improved reading scores after the four months of the project.

In addition they were deriving a sense of accomplishment, and discovering that they could enjoy books. They picked up books at home, and asked to read to their parents. At the same time, it is important to note that this was not a miracle cure. Some of the children retained their gains into the fourth grade, and some did not. We can speculate that without the continuing focused practice and the accompanying special attention, the children with weaker skills were unable to maintain the pace and feel successful in class. They remind us that regular monitoring and extra help need to be maintained until each child is clearly out of the woods.

Collaborative Oral Reading

Curtis and Longo (1999) describe this technique in their work with adolescents who are poor readers. Five or six students and a teacher, each with their own copy of the book, take a turn at reading three to five lines, with turns passed on to anyone in the group in no predetermined order. The unpredictability helps students stay alert, and the reading material is sufficiently sophisticated to interest them, although the reading level matches their abilities. When a novel is read aloud in this way, students see the same words occurring repeatedly, hear the phraseology, and have repeated opportunities to practice in a single session.

Speed Drills

Fischer (1999) has taken a different approach to fluency, attacking the problem at the level of individual words rather than connected text. She constructs one-minute speed drills, giving children a page on which four to seven different words are written, repeated over and over in random sequence. The task must be easy, with the words chosen according to letter-sound elements the child has learned to a reasonable degree of mastery. The goal for each speed drill is to read as many of the words on the page as possible in one minute. Children can work on more than one page of speed drills in a lesson period, and Fischer reports that some work on five to ten at a time. They can keep their own files of current speed drills and the chart for recording times. Fischer notes that in addition to being used in tutorial sessions, "Speed drills with carefully chosen words, with students who can already decode them, for a few minutes a day, can be a very productive addition to a comprehensive reading program" (p. 13).

Spelling and Handwriting

Multisensory instruction by its very nature will include spelling and handwriting activities. Spelling words aloud and writing them are an integral part of almost every program. This is doubly useful because these activities not only strengthen students' ability to identify words when they come across them in print but also are important in teaching spelling and handwriting in their own right.

With rare exceptions, all dyslexics have trouble with

spelling. It stands to reason that they would, because *recalling* the exact image of a word in order to write it down is a more demanding task than *recognizing* it in print. In fact, continuing difficulty with spelling is a common outcome for students who have sufficiently overcome their dyslexia to read comfortably.

Handwriting is a problem for many but not all dyslexics, and for those who do have difficulties, they are as a rule easier to remediate than spelling. This is because handwriting involves learning to master a particular fine motor activity, which is applied to a finite set of symbols. In that way, handwriting and decoding are similar: both deal with a limited set of items to be mastered, and can usually be brought to a successful level of functioning with proper training and sufficient practice. There is remediation for spelling, but it is a longer and more complex process.

Remediation, Compensation, or Accommodation

To close this chapter and the book, we are going to consider some important distinctions between remediation, compensation, and accommodation as they apply to helping people with reading disabilities and related learning problems.

Remediation, a word derived from *remedy*, carries implications of correcting or eliminating a problem and thereby reaching a desired objective. Compensation has to do with reaching the objective by other means within your capabilities, even though you cannot correct or eliminate the problem. Accommodation allows you to reach the objective, but not through your own capabilities; the accommodation is made by someone else.

To take a simple example: you want to walk to the grocery store to buy a loaf of bread. But you cannot do it because you have a very sore foot. There is no immediate *remedy* for the sore foot; it won't be better for several days. You can *compensate* for your inability to walk by driving to the store for the bread, thereby achieving your objective using your own resources. Or you can call the store and ask them to *accommodate* you by delivering the bread to your home.

Here is another example, a little closer to the topic. A blind man cannot read a printed book, and his inability to read print cannot be remediated. He can compensate by learning to read Braille. He has achieved the goal of reading, though not reading through sight. If he does not know Braille, he can turn to an external source—recorded books—which will accommodate his desire to know the content of books.

These distinctions are not always easy to sort out, and sometimes they overlap, but they are very important when parents and schools make educational plans for their children. Remediation is often a long, slow process, and it is tempting to turn to the various means of electronic accommodation that are widely available today. Children having difficulty learning math facts can be encouraged and helped to master them with remedial help, or they can be allowed to use a calculator. Children with poor handwriting can be assisted to develop legible cursive writing, or they can be directed to use computers. Turning to these mechanical aids, which accommodate a learning weakness but do not strengthen truly independent skills, is very tempting, but it is important to keep long-term goals in mind. Writing and performing simple arithmetic calculations without electronic assistance are important skills throughout adult life, and it is a deprivation rather than a gift to stop expecting and assisting schoolchildren to achieve reasonable competence in these areas. Of course, this need not be an either/or matter. A student can use a calculator to complete tonight's homework, and still be working at other times to master math facts and operations. One can use the computer to write a book report, and also be working on developing fluent, useful handwriting. But in my experience, the tendency has been to abandon remediation in these basic skills when a quick and satisfying alternative is available.

Quick electronic fixes for reading are not as readily available in today's world, but there are recorded materials for dyslexic students, and there are parents and teachers reading aloud to children so they can get through their assignments in time for class. There is no objection to these often essential aids. The concern is that they are too frequently used to the exclusion of genuine remedial efforts. In some instances reading disabled children are provided with classroom aides who help them through their schoolwork, but there is no effort to remediate the reading. This is not a simple matter, and decisions have to be made case by case, taking into account other factors, including the severity of the problem, the nature and cost of available resources, and other difficulties a student may have in addition to reading. There are few perfect solutions, but thoughtful and comprehensive planning go a long way.

In many cases, various combinations of remediation, compensation, and accommodation give the best result available. Lorna, the physical therapist discussed in Chapter 5, had compensated for her language difficulties by picturing and acting out the verbal information on the test until she understood it. But she also needed the accommodation of a private room and extended time. Many cases of moderate and severe dyslexia have been effectively remediated to the extent that the students have been able to read anything they come across, but they continue to read more slowly than average. The compensations and accommodations they arrange in their lives then have to do with time management.

Given our current level of knowledge about how children learn to read, what factors impede the process, and how reading disabilities can be overcome, we have it within our means to teach almost every person to read. We know how to help the children. The next step is to help teachers and schools accomplish this fundamental aim of education.

References

Adams, M. J., (1990). *Beginning to read: Thinking and learning about print.* Cambridge, MA: MIT Press.

Adams, M. J., & Bruck, M. (1995). Resolving the "great debate." *American Educator, 19*(2), 7, 10–19.

Adams, M. J., Foorman, B. R., Lundberg, I., & Beeler, T. (1997). *Phonemic awareness in young children: A classroom curriculum.* Baltimore: Paul H. Brookes.

Anderson, K. G. (1997). Gender bias and special education referrals. *Annals of Dyslexia, XLVII,* 151–162.

Balmuth, M. (1982). *The roots of phonics.* New York: Teachers College Press.

Blachman, B. (1996). Preventing early reading failure. In S. C. Cramer & W. Ellis (Eds.), *Learning disabilities: Lifelong issues,* pp. 65–70. Baltimore: Paul H. Brookes.

Bond, G. L., & Dykstra, R. (1967). The cooperative research program in first-grade reading instruction. *Reading Research Quarterly, 3,* 5–142.

Carter, L. F. (1984). The sustaining effects study of compensatory and elementary education. *Educational Researcher 13*(7), 4–13.

Cattell, R. B. (1950). *Personality.* New York: McGraw-Hill.

Catts, H. W., & Kamhi, A. G. (1999). Classification of reading disabilities. In H. W. Catts & A. G. Kamhi (Eds.), *Language and reading disabilities,* pp. 73–94. Boston: Allyn & Bacon.

Chall, J. S. (1983). *Learning to read: The great debate* (Updated ed.). New York: McGraw-Hill.

Chall, J. S. (1996). *Learning to read: The great debate* (3rd ed.). New York: Harcourt Brace & Co.

Chall, J. S. (1997). Are reading methods changing again? *Annals of Dyslexia, 47,* 257–263.

Chall, J. S., & Popp, H. M. (1996). *Teaching and assessing phonics: Why, what, when, how.* Cambridge, MA: Educators Publishing Service.

Chomsky, C. (1978). When you still can't read in third grade: After decoding, what? In S. J. Samuels (Ed.), *What research has to say about reading instruction.* Newark, NJ: International Reading Association.

Clark, D. B., & Urhy, J. K. (1995). *Dyslexia: Theory and practice of remedial instruction*. Baltimore: York Press.

Commission on Reading, National Academy of Education. (1985). *Becoming a nation of readers*. Washington, DC: National Institute of Education.

Cranston-Gringas, A., & Mauser, A. J. (1992). Categorical and non-categorical teacher certification in special education: How wide is the gap? *Remedial and Special Education, 13*(4), 6–9.

Curtis, M. E., & Longo, A. M. (1999). *When adolescents can't read: Methods and materials that work*. Cambridge, MA: Brookline Books.

Dowhower, S. L. (1989). Repeated reading: Research into practice. *The Reading Teacher, 42*, 502–507.

Erikson, E. (1963). *Childhood and society* (2nd ed.). New York: Norton.

Fernald, G. M., & Keller, H. (1921). The effect of kinesthetic factors in development of word recognition in the case of non-readers. *Journal of Educational Research, 4*, 355–377.

Fischer, P. (1999). Getting up to speed. *Perspectives, 25*(2), 12–13.

Flesch, R. (1955 & 1985). *Why Johnny can't read*. New York: Harper & Row.

Fletcher, J. M. (1998). IQ-discrepancy: An inadequate and iatrogenic conceptual model of learning disabilities. *Perspectives, 24*(1), 10–11, 13.

Fletcher, J. M., & Lyon, G. R. (1998). Reading: A research-based approach. In W. M. Evers (Ed.), *What's gone wrong in America's classrooms*, pp. 49–90. Stanford, CA: Hoover Institution Press.

Fodor, J. (1983). *Modularity of mind: A monograph on faculty psychology*. Cambridge, MA: MIT Press.

Foorman, B. R., Francis, D. J., & Fletcher, J. M. (1997). NICHD early intervention project. *Perspectives, 23*(4), 4–5.

Francis, D. J., Shaywitz, S. E., Stuebing, K. K., Shaywitz, B. A., & Fletcher, J. M. (1996). Developmental lag versus deficit models of reading disability: A longitudinal, individual growth curves analysis. *Journal of Educational Psychology, 88*, 3–17.

Frederick, L. D. (1997, September 3). *The key to helping America read*. Report to U.S. House of Representatives Committee on Education and the Workforce.

Fries, C. C. (1963). *Linguistics and reading*. New York: Holt, Rinehart, Winston.

Gersten, R. (1984). Follow through revisited: Reflections on the site variability issue. *Educational Evaluation and Policy Analysis, 6*(4), 411–423.

Gillingham, A., & Stillman, B. (1960). *Remedial training for children with specific disability in reading, writing, and penmanship*. Cambridge, MA: Educators Publishing Service.

Goodman, K. (1967). Reading: A psycholinguistic guessing game. *Journal of the Reading Specialist, 4*, 126–135.

Hammill, D. D. (1990). On defining learning disabilities: An emerging consensus. *Journal of Learning Disabilities, 23*, 74–84.

Henry, M. (1998). The Orton legacy. *Annals of Dyslexia, 48*, 3–26.

Hinshelwood, J. (1917). *Congenital word-blindness*. London: H. K. Lewis.

Hulme, C. (1981). *Reading retardation and multi-sensory teaching*. London: Routledge and Kegan Paul.

James, H. (1902/1965). *The Wings of the Dove*. Baltimore: Penguin Books.

Juel, C. (1988). Learning to read and write: A longitudinal study of 54 children from first through fourth grades. *Journal of Educational Psychology, 80*, 437–447.

Kapp, S., & Kravitz-Zodda, J. (1999). *Reading by the rules* (4th ed.). Burlington, MA: Wisnea-Kapp Reading Programs.

Kawi, A. A., & Pasamenick, B. (1959). Prenatal and paranatal factors in the development of childhood reading disorders. *Monographs of the Society for Research in Child Development, 24*(4).

Kirk, S. A. (1963). Behavioral diagnosis and remediation of learning disabilities. *Proceedings, Conference on Exploration into the Problems of the Perceptually Handicapped Child, Vol. 1.*

Lemann, N. (1997, November). The reading wars. *Atlantic Monthly, 128–134*.

Lemann, N. (1998, November). "Ready, read." *Atlantic Monthly, 92–104*.

Leonhardt, M. (1993). *Parents who love reading, kids who don't*. New York: Crown.

Lerner, J. (1993). *Learning disabilities: Theories, diagnosis & teaching strategies*. Boston: Houghton Mifflin.

Levine, A. (1994, December). The great debate revisited. *Atlantic Monthly*, 38–44.

Lindamood, C. H., & Lindamood, P. C. (1975). *Auditory discrimination in depth*. Allen, TX: DLM Teaching Resources.

Lyon, G. R. (1995). Toward a definition of dyslexia. *Annals of Dyslexia, 45*, 3–27.

Lyon, G. R. (1996). The state of research. In S. C. Cramer & W. Ellis (Eds.), *Learning disabilities: Lifelong issues*, pp. 3–61. Baltimore: Paul H. Brookes.

Lyon, G. R. (1997, July 10). *Learning to read*. Report to U.S. House of Representatives Committee on Education and the Workforce.

Lyon, G. R. (1998, March). Why reading is not a natural process. *Educational Leadership*, 14–18.

Lyon, G. R. (1998, April 28). *Overview of reading and literacy initiatives*. Report to U.S. Senate Committee on Labor and Human Resources.

Lyon, G. R., & Alexander, D. (1996–1997). NICHD research program in learning disabilities. *Their World*, 13–15.

Lyon, G. R., & Chhabra, V. (1996). The current state of science and the future of specific reading disability. *Mental Retardation and Developmental Disabilities Research Reviews, 2*, 2–9.

Moats, L. C. (1995a). *Spelling: Development, disability, and instruction*. Baltimore: York Press.

Moats, L. C. (1995b). The missing foundation in teacher education. *American Educator, 19*(2), 9, 43–51.

Moats, L. C. (1997, September 3). *Hearing on teachers: The key to helping America read*. Statement before the U.S. House of Representatives Committee on Education and the Workforce.

Morgan, W. P. (1896). A case of congenital word-blindness. *British Medical Journal, 2,* 1378.

Needlman, R. (1997). *Pediatric interventions to prevent reading problems in young children.* Paper written for the Committee on the Prevention of Reading Difficulties in Young Children, National Research Council. *New York Times.* (1997, January 25).

Olivier, C., & Bowler, R. F. (1996). *Learning to learn.* New York: Simon & Schuster.

Pennington, B. (1991). *Diagnosing learning disorders: A neuropsychological framework.* New York: Guilford Press.

Puma, M., Karweit, N., Price, C., Ricciuti, A., Thompson, W., & Vaden-Kiernan, M. (1997). *Prospects: Final report on student outcomes.* Washington, DC: U.S. Department of Education, Planning and Evaluation Services.

Ryan, M. (1999, August 8). They help bring stories to life. *Parade Magazine, 8.*

Samuels, S. J. (1979). The method of repeated readings. *The Reading Teacher, 32,* 403–408.

Sanders, M. (1979). *Clinical assessment of learning problems.* Boston: Allyn & Bacon.

Sever, J. L. (1986). Perinatal infections and damage to the central nervous system. In M. Lewis (Ed.), *Learning disabilities and prenatal risk,* pp. 194–209. Urbana-Champaign, IL: University of Illinois Press.

Shankweiler, D. (1999). Comprehension and decoding: Patterns of association in children with reading difficulties. *Scientific Studies of Reading, 3*(1), 69–94.

Siegel, L. S. (1989). IQ is irrelevant to the definition of learning disabilities. *Journal of Learning Disabilities, 22,* 469–478.

Slavin, R. E., Karweit, N. L., Wasik, B. A., Madden, N. A., & Dolan, L. J. (1994). Success for All: A comprehensive approach to prevention and early intervention. In R. E. Slavin, N. L. Karweit, & B. A. Wasik (Eds.), *Preventing early school failure: Research, policy, and practice,* pp. 175–205. Boston: Allyn & Bacon.

Smith, N. B. (1965). *American reading instruction.* Newark, DE: International Reading Association.

Snow, C. E., Burns, M. S., & Griffin, P. (Eds.) (1998). *Preventing reading difficulties in young children.* Washington, DC: National Academy Press.

Stanovich, K. E. (1986). Matthew effects in reading: Some consequences of individual differences in the acquisition of literacy. *Reading Research Quarterly, 21,* 360–406.

Stanovich, K. E. (1992). Speculations on the causes and consequences of individual differences in early reading acquisition. In P. B. Gough, L. C. Ehri, R. Treiman (Eds.), *Reading acquisition,* pp. 307–342. Hillsdale, NJ: Lawrence Erlbaum.

Stanovich, K. E., Cunningham, A. E., & Feeman, D. J. (1984). Intelligence, cognitive skills and early reading progress. *Reading Research Quarterly, 19,* 278–303.

Stanovich, K., & Siegel, L. S. (1994). Phenotypic performance profiles of children with reading disabilities: A regression-based test of the phonological-core variable-difference model. *Journal of Educational Psychology, 86,* 24–53.

Stegner, W. (1937/1996). *Remembering laughter.* New York: Penguin Books.

Streissguth, A. P. (1986). Smoking and drinking during pregnancy and offspring learning disabilities: A review of the literature and development of a research strategy. In M. Lewis (Ed.), *Learning disabilities and prenatal risk,* pp. 28–67. Champaign-Urbana, IL: University of Illinois Press.

Torgesen, J. K. (1997). Research on the prevention and remediation of phonologically based reading disabilities. *Perspectives, 23*(4), 27–28.

Torgesen, J. K. (1999). Assessment and instruction for phonemic awareness and word recognition skills. In H. W. Catts & A. G. Kamhi (Eds.), *Language and reading disabilities,* pp. 128–153. Boston: Allyn & Bacon.

Torgesen, J., Wagner, R., & Rashotte, C. (1999). *Test of Word Reading Efficiency (TOWRE).* Austin, TX: PRO-ED.

U.S. Office of Education. (1968). *First Annual Report of the National Advisory Committee on Handicapped Children.* Washington, DC: U.S. Department of Health, Education, and Welfare.

Venezky, R. L. (1975). The curious role of letter names in reading instruction. *Visible Language, 9,* 7–23.

Werner, H. (1957a). *The comparative psychology of mental development* (Rev. ed.). New York: International Universities Press.

Werner, H. (1957b). The concept of development from a comparative and organismic point of view. In S. S. Barten & M. B. Franklin (Eds.), *Developmental processes: Heinz Werner's selected writings, 1,* pp. 107–130. New York: International Universities Press.

Worthy, J., Moorman, M., & Turner, M. (1999). What Johnny likes to read is hard to find in school. *Reading Research Quarterly, 34*(1), 12–27.

Glossary

Alphabetic Principle The system of using alphabet letters to represent the sequence of sounds in words.

Automaticity A process by which an activity, in this instance the mechanical aspect of reading, has become so well learned and routinized that it does not require conscious attention.

Cognitive Abilities The various and somewhat discrete skills that make up general intelligence.

Consonant Blends Two or three consonants occurring together, with each one voiced, as in plan (you hear the /p/ and the /l/) and struck (you hear the /s/,/t/, and /r/).

Decoding The process of analyzing a word according to the sounds represented by its component letters. It is one method of *word identification* (the other principal method being whole word recognition).

Digraph Two successive letters representing a single sound—for example, *ch*.

Direct Phonics Instruction Also referred to as explicit instruction. Sound-symbol relationships are taught in a planned sequence, during lessons dedicated to that activity. (Compare with *indirect phonics instruction.*)

Dyslexia Literally, faulty reading. In this book, the term indicates "pure dyslexia"—that is, difficulty in word identification. See also Appendix A.

Grapheme A letter or group of letters representing a single speech sound—for example, *igh*.

Indirect Phonics Instruction Also known as embedded or opportunistic instruction, it is the practice of teaching the phonics code by helping children sound out words as they come upon them in text, rather than in separate, explicit, sequential lessons.

Kinesthetic Pertaining to kinesthesia, the awareness of muscle movement.

Mnemonic Pertaining to memory. Sometimes used as a noun, as in "We invented a mnemonic to help her remember the name of that letter."

Modular Systems In the context of reading, mental abilities such as perception and memory, which can function independently of other mental abilities or general intelligence.

NICHD National Institute of Child Health and Human Development. The government agency that has directed the research on reading instruction and reading difficulties. One of the National Institutes of Health.

Orthography The spelling system of a written language.

Phoneme The smallest unit of spoken language.

Phonics A method of teaching reading that stresses the learning and use of symbol-sound connections.

Phonology Units of sound in spoken language, including phonemes, syllables, and rhymes.

Public Law 94-142 The first comprehensive federal legislation guaranteeing the rights of all children with disabilities to an appropriate, publicly supported education. First passed in 1975, it has since been renamed the Individuals with Disabilities Education Act (IDEA).

Sight Words Words recognized as wholes, rather than through decoding or sounding out. Also referred to as look-say words.

Spelling-to-Sound Correspondence (Also referred to as *symbol-sound correspondence*) The relationship between graphic symbols and the sounds they represent. This is the same relationship indicated when one talks about *paired associates* in learning the code.

Stages I, II, III See Werner stages of mental development.

Syntax Sentence structure or, more explicitly, the part of grammar dealing with the relationship of words to each other.

Werner Stages of Mental Development
Stage I—global, whole qualities dominate perception.
Stage II—analytic, with perception directed toward parts.
Stage III—integrated, with parts perceived in relation to each other and to the whole.

APPENDIX A

Definitions of Dyslexia and Learning Disabilities

DEFINITIONS OF DYSLEXIA FROM THE INTERNATIONAL DYSLEXIA ASSOCIATION

I. Research Committee Definition, May 1994

Dyslexia is one of several distinct learning disabilities. It is a specific language-based disorder of constitutional origin characterized by difficulties in single word decoding usually reflecting insufficient phonological processing abilities. These difficulties in single word decoding are often unexpected in relation to age and other cognitive and academic abilities; they are not the result of generalized developmental disability or sensory impairment. Dyslexia is manifested by variable difficulty with different forms of language, often including, in addition to problems in reading, a conspicuous problem with acquiring proficiency in writing and spelling.

(Note: The IDA Research Committee's definition has been adopted by the National Institute of Child Health and Human Development (NICHD) for its research programs in dyslexia and learning disabilities.)

II. Members Committee Definition, November 1994

Dyslexia is a neurologically-based, often familial, disorder that interferes with the acquisition and processing of language. Varying in degrees of severity, it is manifested by difficulties in receptive and expressive language, including phonological processing, reading, writing, spelling, handwriting, and sometimes arithmetic. Dyslexia is not a result of lack of motivation, sensory impairment, inadequate instructional or environmental opportunities, or other limiting conditions, but may occur together with these conditions. Although dyslexia is life-long, individuals with dyslexia frequently respond successfully to timely and appropriate intervention.

Both definitions of dyslexia are reprinted with permission from the International Dyslexia Association quarterly newsletter, *Perspectives*, 1998 (4), 4.

DEFINITIONS OF LEARNING DISABILITY

I. Federal Government Definition, 1968

Children with specific learning disabilities exhibit a *disorder* in one or more of the basic psychological processes involved in understanding or in using spoken or written language. These may be manifested in disorders of listening, thinking, talking, reading, writing, spelling, or arithmetic. They include conditions that have been referred to as perceptual handicaps, brain injury, minimal brain dysfunction, dyslexia, developmental aphasia, etc. They do not include learning problems that are due primarily to visual, hearing, or motor handicaps, to mental retardation, emotional disturbance, or to environmental disadvantage (U.S. Office of Education, 1968, 34).

II. National Joint Committee on Learning Disabilities (NJCLD) Definition, 1988

Learning disabilities is a general term that refers to a heterogeneous group of disorders manifested by significant difficulty in the acquisition and use of listening, speaking, reading, writing, reasoning, or mathematical abilities. These disorders are intrinsic to the individual, presumed to be due to central nervous system dysfunction, and may occur across the life span. Problems in self-regulatory behavior, social perception, and social interaction may exist with learning disabilities but do not by themselves constitute a learning disability. Although learning disabilities may occur concomitantly with other handicapping conditions (sensory impairment, mental retardation, social and emotional disturbance) or with extrinsic influences (cultural differences, insufficient or inappropriate instruction), they are not the result of these conditions.

APPENDIX B

Resources for Parents and Teachers

BOOKS AND MATERIALS

Adams, Marilyn J., Foorman, Barbara R., Lundberg, Ingvar, & Beeler, Terri
Phonemic Awareness in Young Children: A Classroom Curriculum. Baltimore: Paul H. Brookes, 1998.

Beck, Isabel L., & Juel, Connie
"The Role of Decoding in Learning to Read" In S. J. Samuels and A. E. Farstrup (Eds.), *What Research Has to Say About Reading Instruction.* Newark, NJ: International Reading Association, 1992.

Chall, Jeanne S., & Popp, Helen M.
Teaching and Assessing Phonics: Why, What, When, How. Cambridge, MA: Educators Publishing Service, 1996.

Davis, Robin Works
Toddle on Over: Developing Infant & Toddler Literature Programs. Fort Atkinson, WI: Alleyside Press, 1998.

Heilman, Arthur W.
Phonics in Proper Perspective. Upper Saddle River, NJ: Prentice Hall, 1998.

Honig, Bill
Teaching Our Children to Read: The Role of Skills in a Comprehensive Reading Program. Thousand Oaks, CA: Corwin Press, 1996.

Leonhardt, Mary
99 Ways to Get Kids to Love Reading, and 100 Books They'll Love. New York: Three Rivers Press, 1997.

LinguiSystems, Inc.
  Reading Specialist Catalog. 3100 4th Avenue, East Moline, IL 61244-9700. 800-776-4322. E-mail: linguisys@aol.com
Meltzer, Lynn, & Solomon, Bethany
  Educational Prescriptions for the Classroom for Students with Learning Problems. Cambridge, MA: Educators Publishing Service, 1988.
Moats, Louisa C.
  Spelling: Development, Disability, and Instruction. Baltimore, MD: York Press, 1995.
Olivier, Carolyn, & Bowler, Rosemary F.
  Learning to Learn. New York: Simon & Schuster, 1996.
Sedita, Joan
  Study Skills Guide. Prides Crossing, MA: Landmark Foundation, 1989.

ORGANIZATIONS AND THEIR PUBLICATIONS AND WEBSITES

International Dyslexia Association (IDA) Formerly Orton Dyslexia Society
8600 LaSalle Road, Suite 382
Baltimore, MD 21204-6020
(410) 296-0232
Website: www.interdys.org

Annual Publication: *Annals of Dyslexia.* A scholarly journal of articles covering research into causes and treatment of dyslexia, theoretical discussions, and teaching programs.
Quarterly Publication: *Perspectives.* A newsletter geared primarily for parents and teachers, containing opinion pieces, book reviews, news of meetings and conferences, announcements of workshops, and other timely articles and information.

National Center for Learning Disabilities (NCLD)
381 Park Avenue South, Suite 1420
New York, NY 10016
(212) 545-7510
Website: www.ncld.org

Annual Publication: *Their World.* A magazine directed mainly toward parents and teachers that offers summaries of recent research information; personal experiences of parents, teachers, and students; and articles on current trends in learning disabilities and special education.

Parent-Child Home Program
585 Plandome Road, Suite 105B
Manhasset, New York 11030
Website: www.parent-child.org

This program provides training at home for parents who want to help their young children develop a love of books and strong literacy skills.

Hello Friend / Ennis William Cosby Foundation
Website: www.hellofriend.org

The foundation offers excellent guidelines to teachers and parents of children with learning difficulties, as well as other information about learning differences.

Index